Life

of

Saint Columba,

2

Life

of

Saint Columba,

FOUNDER OF HY.

WRITTEN BY ADAMNAN,

NINTH ABBOT OF THAT MONASTERY.

EDITED BY

WILLIAM REEVES, D.D., M.R.I.A.,

RECTOR OF TYNAN, AND CANON OF ARMAGH.

Facsimile reprint 1988 by Llanerch Enterprises, Llanerch, Felinfach, Lampeter, Dyfed. SA48 8PJ. Reprinted from the HISTORIANS OF SCOTLAND, Edmonston and Douglas, 1874. Readers seeking further background information are referred to the extensive academic notes in that edition.

ISBN 0947992197

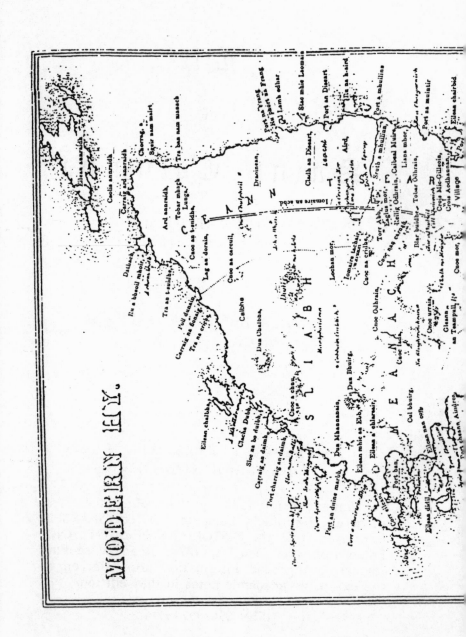

MODERN HY.

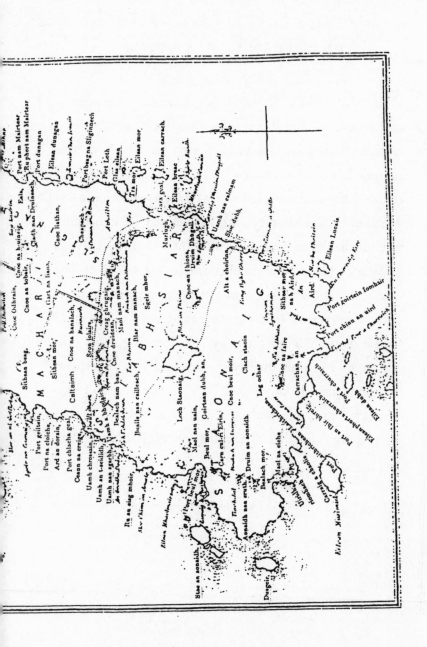

PRELIMINARY NOTICE.

THE Life of St. Columba by Adamnan has always excited much interest, from the undoubted authenticity of the Biography, the early period in which it was compiled, and its connexion with the foundation of the ecclesiastical establishment at Iona, and the introduction of Christianity into the north of Scotland; but until the appearance, in 1856, of Dr. Reeves's edition of the Life, its real character, and that of the establishment at Iona, was little understood, and its history perverted to suit the purposes of a polemical controversy. The accuracy of learning and the thorough research displayed in Dr. Reeves's edition has now placed the subject beyond the reach of controversy, and his truly admirable edition is accompanied by a wealth of illustration almost unrivalled.

TABLE OF CONTENTS.

BOOK II.

ON HIS MIRACULOUS POWERS.

PREFACE.

BEFORE St. Columba was long in the grave, it is likely that some member of the brotherhood set himself to collect his patron's acts, and to record such events of his life as were suited to the taste of the day, or were calculated to promote the veneration of his memory. In furtherance of this design, he probably turned his attention rather to the marvels than the sober realities of the Saint's life, and consulted more for the excitement of admiration in a simple and credulous age, than for the supply of historical materials to meet the stern demands of remote posterity. When Adamnan, a century after St. Columba's death, in compliance with his brethren's urgent request, drew up the memoir which has immortalized both the subject and the writer, his information was derived, as he himself states, in part from written, in part from oral, authorities. In the latter respect, he was quite near enough to the fountain-head, both in time and place, to draw from authentic sources, for in his boyhood he had frequent opportunities of conversing with those who had seen St. Columba, and he was now writing almost on the very spot where his great predecessor had indited his last words, and surrounded by objects every one of which was fresh with the impress of some interesting association. As regarded his documentary materials, he had before him the account of Çummæne the Fair, whom he cites by name, and whose entire narrative he has transferred, almost verbatim, into his own compilation, where it is for the most part incorporated with the Third Book. He had also another memoir, on the authority of which he relates an occurrence not recorded in

Cummene's pages. Besides these compositions, which were written in Latin, there existed in our author's day certain poems on the praises of Columba, in the Scotic tongue, among which was probably the celebrated *Amhra*, or panegyric, which was written by a contemporary of the Saint. Baithene Mor, who enjoyed St. Columba's friendship, is said to have commemorated some particulars of his life, and poems ascribed to Baithene are more than once referred to by O'Donnell. Metrical compositions bearing the name of St. Mura are also cited by the same compiler, who adduces them as his authority, in part, for the history of St. Columba's infancy. Thus furnished with record and tradition, and quickened, moreover, with zeal for the honour of a kinsman after the flesh, the ninth abbot of Hy became the biographer of the first, and produced a work, which, though not ostensibly historical, and professing to treat of an individual, is "the most authentic voucher now remaining of several other important particulars of the sacred and civil history of the Scots and Picts,"[1] and is pronounced by a writer not over-given to eulogy to be "the most complete piece of such biography that all Europe can boast of, not only at so early a period, but even through the whole middle ages."[2]

---

[1] Innes, Civil and Eccl. Hist., p. 145.
[2] Pinkerton, Enquiry, Pref., vol. ʿ. p. xlviii.

INTRODUCTION.

I.

Sᴛ. Cᴏʟᴜᴍʙᴀ was born at Gartan, a wild district in the Cʜʀᴏɴᴏ-
ʟᴏɢɪᴄᴀʟ
Sᴜᴍᴍᴀʀʏ
ᴏꜰ Sᴀɪɴᴛ
Cᴏʟᴜᴍʙᴀ'ꜱ
Lɪꜰᴇ.
county of Donegal, on the very day that St. Buite, the founder
of Monasterboice, departed this life. Thus the 7th of December
is determined for an event, the date of which might otherwise
have been unrecorded; and the Irish Calendars, in noticing
it, present at that day the anomaly of a secular commemoration. Authorities vary as to the year, ranging from 518 to
523; but calculation from Adamnan's data gives 521 as that
most likely to be the true period.

Fedhlimidh, the father of Columba, belonged to the clan
which occupied, and gave name to, the territory surrounding
Gartan, and was, moreover, a member of the reigning families
of Ireland and British Dalriada. Eithne, the mother of
Columba, was of Leinster extraction, and descended from an
illustrious provincial king. Thus the nobility of two races was
combined in their son, and, no doubt, contributed to the
extended influence which he acquired, when education, piety,
and zeal were superadded to his honourable antecedents.

He was baptized by the presbyter Cruithnechan, under the
name *Colum*, to which the addition of *cille*, signifying " of
the church," was subsequently made, in reference to his diligent attendance at the church of his youthful sojourn. The
tradition of the country is, that he was baptized at Tulach-
Dubhglaise, now called Temple-Douglas, a place about half-

way between Gartan and Letterkenny, where there is a cemetery of considerable extent, containing the roofless walls of a large chapel, and, at a short distance on the north-east, within the enclosure, a square, elevated space, which appears to have been artificially formed, and to be the spot which in O'Donnell's time was coupled with the memory of the Saint.

The place where St. Columba is said to have spent the principal portion of his boyhood was Doire-Eithne, a hamlet in the same territory, which afterwards exchanged this name, signifying, *Roboretum Eithneæ*, for *Cill-mac-Nenain*, in commemoration, it is supposed, of the "Sons of Enan," whose mother was one of St. Columba's sisters. The absence of any mention of this place in the ancient Irish Life, coupled with the fact that this parish was the original seat of the O'Donnells, might suggest the conjecture, that it was introduced into the biography of the Saint as an expedient of a later age to add lustre to the chiefs of Tirconnell, by associating the history of their patron with the origin of their race, were it not that there is evidence of a very early relation between St. Columba's family and the place, in the circumstance that the O'Freels, who were the ancient herenachs of the church lands there, were descended, not from Dalach, the forefather of the O'Donnells, but from Eoghan, the brother of St. Columba. The name Cill-mac-Nenain, also, as explained above, indicates a like connexion.

The youth Columba, when arrived at sufficient age, left the scene of his fosterage, and, travelling southwards, came to Moville, at the head of Strangford Lough, where he became a pupil of the famous bishop, St. Finnian. Here he was ordained deacon; and to the period of his sojourn in this monastery is referable the anecdote which is told by Adamnan in the opening chapter of the second book.

From Moville, St. Columba proceeded further southwards, and, arriving in Leinster, placed himself under the instruction of an aged bard called Gemman. At this stage of the Saint's life, he being still a deacon, occurred an incident which Adamnan records in the course of his narrative (B. II. c. 26).

Leaving Gemman, he entered the monastic seminary of Clonard, over which St. Finnian, the founder, then presided. Here St. Columba is said to have been numbered with a class of students who afterwards attained great celebrity as fathers of the Irish Church. St. Finnian does not appear to have been a bishop, and when Columba was subsequently judged worthy of admission to superior orders, he was sent to Etchen, the bishop of Clonfad, by whom he was ordained a priest.

According to the Irish memoirs, St. Columba left St. Finnian, and entered the monastery of Mobhi Claraine ch, whose establishment at Glas Naoidhen, now Glasnevin, near Dublin, consisted of a group of huts or cells, and an oratory, situate on either bank of the Finglass. Here also are said to have been, at the same time, SS. Comgall, Ciaran, and Cainnech, who had been his companions at Clonard. A violent distemper, however, which appeared in the neighbourhood about 544, broke up the community, and Columba returned to the north. On his way he crossed the Bior, now called the Moyola water, a small river which runs into Lough Neagh on the north-west, and, in doing so, prayed, it is said, that this might be the northern limit to the spread of the disease. Mobhi died in 545, and in the following year, according to the Annals of Ulster, the church of Derry was founded by St. Columba, he being then twenty-five years of age. In 549 his former teacher, St. Finnian of Clonard, was removed from this life.

About the year 553, he founded the monastery of Durrow, of which, as his chief institution in Ireland, Bede makes special mention. We have no means of ascertaining the dates of his other churches; and all we can do with any probability is to allow generally the fifteen years' interval between 546 and 562 for their foundation.

In 561 was fought the battle of Cooldrevny, which is believed to have been, in a great measure, brought about at St. Columba's instigation. A synod, which Adamnan states (B. III. c. 4) was assembled to excommunicate St. Columba, met at Teltown, in Meath, probably at the instance of the sovereign who was worsted in the battle; for Teltown was in the heart of his patrimonial territory, and was one of his royal seats. The assembly, however, was not unanimous, and St. Brendan of Birr protested against the sentence. St. Finnian of Moville, also, soon after testified his sense of veneration for the accused, who had been once his pupil (B. III. c. 5).

Whether the censure which was expressed against St. Columba by the majority of the clergy had, or could have had, any influence on his after course, is difficult to determine. Irish accounts say that St. Molaisi of Devenish, or of Inish-murry, was the arbiter of his future lot, who imposed upon him the penance of perpetual exile from his native country. But this seems to be a legendary creation of a later age, when missionary enterprise was less characteristic of Irish ecclesiastics than in St. Columba's day. In removing to Hy, he did no more than Donnan, Maelrubha, and Moluoc voluntarily performed, and Cainnech wished to do. Scotland was then a wide field for clerical exertion, and St. Columba's permanent establishment in one of its outposts, within a day's sail of his native province, entailed very little more self-denial than was required for the repeated and, perhaps, protracted visits of St. Finbar, St. Comgall, St. Brendan, the two Fillans, St. Ronan, St. Flannan, and many others. It was a more decided, and therefore a more successful course than theirs; but it was equally voluntary: at least, there is high authority for supposing it to have been such. "Pro Christo peregrinari volens, enavigavit," the common formula of missionary enterprise, is Adamnan's statement of his motive (Pref. 2): with which Bede's expression, "ex quo ipse prædicaturus abiit" (Hist. Ec. iii. 4), is in perfect keeping. That he returned more than once, and took an active part in civil and religious transactions, is demonstrable from Adamnan. How much oftener he revisited Ireland is not recorded ; but these two instances are quite sufficient to disprove the perpetuity of his retirement. That he was not banished by secular influence is clear even from the legend which represents his dismissal as an ecclesiastical penalty. Early in the next century, St. Carthach, or Mochuda, was driven by the secular arm from his flourishing monastery of Rahen ; but then he only changed his province, and established himself at Lismore. In doing so, however, he took his fraternity with him, and gave up all connexion with Rahen. But St. Columba, when he departed, severed no ties, surrendered no jurisdiction ; his congregations remained in their various settlements, still subject to his authority, and he took with him no more than the prescriptive attendance of a missionary leader.

Durrow, his principal Irish monastery, lay close to the territory of the prince whose displeasure he is supposed to have incurred, yet it remained undisturbed ; and when, at a later time, he revisited Ireland to adjust the affairs of this house, it seemed a fitting occasion for him to traverse Meath, and visit Clonmacnois, the chief foundation of his alleged persecutor, and the religious centre of his family. Surely, if the Northern Hy Neill had defeated King Diarmait, they could easily have sheltered their kinsman.

In 563, St. Columba, now in his forty-second year, passed over with twelve attendants to the west of Scotland, possibly on the invitation of the provincial king, to whom he was allied by blood. Adamnan relates some particulars of an interview which they had this same year (B. I. c. 7) ; and the Irish Annals record the donation of Hy, as the result of King Conall's approval. At this time the island of Hy seems to have been on the confines of the Pictish and Scotic jurisdiction, so that while its tenure was in a measure subject to the consent of either people, it formed a most convenient centre for religious intercourse with both. The Scots were already Christians in name ; the Picts were not. Hence the conversion of the latter formed a grand project for the exercise of missionary exertion, and St. Columba

at once applied himself to the task. He visited the king at his
fortress; and having surmounted the difficulties which at first
lay in his way, he won his esteem, overcame the opposition of
his ministers, and eventually succeeded in planting Christianity
on a permanent footing in their province. The possession of
Hy was formally granted, or substantially confirmed, by this
sovereign also; and the combined consent to the occupation of
it by St. Columba seems to have materially contributed to its
stability as a monastic institution. St. Columba afterwards
paid several visits to the king, whose friendship and co-opera-
tion continued unchanged till his death.

In 573, St. Brendan, of Birr, the friend and admirer of St.
Columba, died, and a festival was instituted at Hy by St.
Columba in commemoration of his day.

Of the places where St. Columba founded churches in Scotland,
Adamnan has preserved some names, as *Ethica insula*, *Elena*,
Himba, *Scia*, but he has given no dates, so that their origin
must be collectively referred to the period of thirty-four years,
ending in 597, during which the Saint was an *insulanus miles*.

Conall, the lord of Dalriada, died in 574, whereupon his cousin,
Aidan, assumed the sovereignty, and was formally inaugurated
by St. Columba in the monastery of Hy. Next year they both
attended the convention of Drumceatt, where the claims of the
Irish king to the homage of British Dalriada were abandoned,
and the independence of that province declared.

St. Brendan, of Clonfert, who had been a frequent visitor of
the western isles, and on one occasion had been a guest of St.
Columba in Himba, died in 577; and St. Finnian of Moville,
also one of our Saint's preceptors, was removed by death in 579.
About the same time a question arose between St. Columba and
St. Comgall, concerning a church in the neighbourhood of Coleraine, which was taken up by their respective races, and engaged
them in sanguinary strife. In 587 another battle was fought,
namely, at Cuilfedha, near Clonard, in which engagement also
St. Columba is said to have been an interested party.

In judging of the martial propensities of St. Columba, it will always be necessary to bear in mind the complexion of the times in which he was born, and the peculiar condition of society in his day, which required even women to enter battle, and justified ecclesiastics in the occasional exercise of warfare. Moreover, if we may judge from the biographical records which have descended to us, primitive Irish ecclesiastics, and especially the superior class, commonly known as saints, were very impatient of contradiction, and very resentful of injury. Excommunication, fasting against, and cursing, were in frequent employment, and inanimate, as well as animate objects, are represented as the subjects of their maledictions. St. Columba, who seems to have inherited the high bearing of his race, was not disposed to receive injuries, or even affronts, in silence. Adamnan relates how he pursued a plunderer with curses, following the retiring boat into the sea, until the water reached to his knees. We have an account also of his cursing a miser who neglected to extend hospitality to him. On another occasion, in Himba, he excommunicated some plunderers of the church; and one of them afterwards perished in combat, being transfixed by a spear which was discharged in St. Columba's name. Possibly some current stories of the Saint's imperious and vindictive temper may have suggested to Venerable Bede the qualified approbation "*qualiscumque fuerit ipse*, nos hoc de illo certum tenemus, quia reliquit successores magna continentia ac divino amore regularique institutione insignes."[1] With the profound respect in which his memory was held, there seems to have been always associated a considerable degree of awe. Hence, perhaps, the repulsive form in which he was supposed to have presented himself to Alexander II. in 1249. Fordun (Bower) tells a story of some English pirates, who stripped the church of Æmonia or Inchcolum, and on their return, being upset, went down like lead to the bottom; upon which he observes: " Qua

---

[1] Beda, Hist. Eccl., iii. 4.

de re versum est in Anglia proverbium; Sanctum viz. Colum-
bam in suos malefactores vindicem fore satis et ultorem. Et
ideo, ut non reticeam quid de eo dicatur, apud eos vulgariter
Sanct Quhalme nuncupatur." [1]

St. Columba visited Ireland subsequently to June 585, and
from Durrow proceeded westwards to Clonmacnois, where he
was received with the warmest tokens of affection and respect.

In 593 he seems to have been visited with sickness, and to
have been brought near death. Such, at least, may be supposed
to be the moral of his alleged declaration concerning the angels
who were sent to conduct his soul to paradise, and whose services were postponed for four years. At length, however, the
day came, and just after midnight, between Saturday the 8th,
and Sunday the 9th of June, in the year 597, while on his knees at
the altar, without ache or struggle, his spirit gently took its flight.

Of his various qualities, both mental and bodily, Adamnan
gives a brief but expressive summary. Writing was an employment to which he was much devoted. Adamnan makes special
mention of books written by his hand; but from the way in
which they are introduced, one would be disposed to conclude
that the exercise consisted in transcription rather than composition. Three Latin hymns of considerable beauty are attributed
to him, and in the ancient *Liber Hymnorum*, where they are
preserved, each is accompanied by a preface describing the
occasion on which it was written. His alleged Irish compositions are also poems: some specimens of which will be found
in the original edition, pp. 264-277, 285-289. There are also
in print his " Farewel to Aran," a poem of twenty-two stanzas;[2]
and another poem of seventeen stanzas, which he is supposed to
have written on the occasion of his flight from King Diarmait.[3]
Besides these, there is a collection of some fifteen poems, bearing
his name, in one of the O'Clery MSS. preserved in the Burgundian

---

[1] Scotichron., xiii. 37.
[2] Transactions of the Gaelic Society, pp. 180-189.
[3] Misc. Ir. Ar. Soc., pp. 3-15.

Library at Brussels. But much the largest collection is contained in an oblong manuscript of the Bodleian library at Oxford, Laud 615, which embraces everything in the shape of poem or fragment that could be called Columba's, which industry was able to scrape together at the middle of the sixteenth century. Many of the poems are ancient, but in the whole collection there is probably not one of Columcille's composition. Among them are his alleged prophecies, the genuineness of which even Colgan called in question. Copies of some of these compositions have been preserved in Ireland, and from a modernized, interpolated, and often garbled version of them, a collection of "the Prophecies of St. Columbkille" has been lately published in Dublin (in 1856). But it is to be regretted that the editor, not content with mediæval forgeries, has lent his name, and, what is worse, has degraded that of St. Columba, to the propagation of a silly imposture, which does not possess even an antiquity of ten years to take off the gloss of its barefaced pretensions.

II.

The belief was current among the Irish at a very early period, that the withdrawal of St. Columba to Britain was a sort of penance, which was, with his own consent, imposed upon him in consequence of his having fomented domestic feuds that resulted in sanguinary engagements. And the opinion derives considerable support, at least as regards the battle of Cul-dreimhne, from the mention of it by Adamnan, who in two instances makes it a kind of Hegira in the Saint's life. The following narrative from Keating's History affords the simplest statement of the prevalent belief :— BATTLES WITH WHICH SAINT COLUMBA WAS CONNECTED

"Now this is the cause why Molaise sentenced Columcille to go into Alba, because it came of him to occasion three battles in Erin, viz., the battle of Cul Dreimhne, the battle of Rathan, and the battle of Cuil Feadha. The cause of the battle of Cul Feadha, according to the old book called the Leabar Uidhre of Ciaran, Diarmuid, son of Fergus Cerrbhoil, king of Ireland, made the Feast of Tara, and a noble man was killed at that feast by Curnan, son of

Aodh, son of Eochuidh Tiorm-carna; wherefore Diarmuid killed him in revenge for that, because he committed murder at the feast of Tara, against law and the sanctuary of the feast; and before Curnan was put to death he fled to the protection of Columcille, and notwithstanding the protection of Columcille he was killed by Diarmuid. And from that it arose that Columcille mustered the Clanna Neill of the North, because his own protection and the protection of the sons of Earc was violated : whereupon the battle of Cuile Dreimhne was gained over Diarmuid and over the Connaghtmen, so that they were defeated through the prayer of Columcille.

"The Black Book of Molaga assigns another cause why the battle of Cul Dreimhne was fought, viz., in consequence of the false judgment which Diarmuid gave against Columcille when he wrote the gospel out of the book of Finnian without his knowledge. Finnian said that it was to himself belonged the son-book [copy] which was written from his book, and they both selected Diarmuid as judge between them. This is the decision that Diarmuid made : that to every book belongs its son-book [copy], as to every cow belongs her calf. So that this is one of the two causes why the battle of Cuile Dreimhne was fought.

"This was the cause which brought Columcille to be induced to fight the battle of Cuil Rathan against the Dal n-Araidhe, and against the Ultonians, viz., in consequence of the controversy that took place between Colum and Comgall, because they took part against Colum in that controversy.

"This was the cause that occasioned the fighting of the battle of Cuil Feadha against Colman Mac Diarmada, viz., in revenge for his having been outraged in the case of Baodan, son of Ninneadh (king of Erin), who was killed by Cuimin, son of Colman, at Leiman-eich, in violation of the sanctuary of Colum." [1]

The book which St. Columba is supposed to have transcribed from St. Finnian's original is not a manuscript of the Gospels, as stated in the above extract, but the copy of the Psalms, which forms, with its silver case, the ancient reliquary called the Cathach, of which O'Donnell gives us this curious account:

"Now *The Cathach* is the name of the book on account of which the battle was fought, and it is the chief relic of Colum-cille in the territory of Cinel Conaill Gulban ; and it is covered with silver under gold; and it is not lawful to open it; and if it be sent

[1] For the original Irish of this and other passages given in the translation only, see Dr. Reeves's Additional Notes to the original Edition.—W. F. S.

thrice, right-wise, around the army of the Cinell Conaill, when they are going to battle, they will return safe with victory : and it is on the breast of a cowarb or a cleric, who is to the best of his power free from mortal sin, that the Cathach should be, when brought round the army."

The record of the battle in the Annals of the Four Masters, at the year 555, is as follows :—

"The seventeenth year of Diarmaid. The battle of Cul-Dreimhne was gained against Diarmaid, son of Cearbhall, by Fearghus and Domhnall, the two sons of Muircheartach, son of Earca ; by Ainmire, son of Sedna ; and by Nainnidh, son of Duach ; and by Aedh, son of Eochaidh Tirmcharna, king of Connaught. It was in revenge of the killing of Curnan, son of Aedh, son of Eochaidh Tirmcharna, while under the protection of Colum-cille, that the Clanna Neill of the North and the Connaughtmen gave this battle of Cul-Dreimhne to King Diarmaid ; and also on account of the false sentence which Diarmaid passed against Colum-cille about a book of Finnen, which Colum had transcribed without the knowledge of Finnen, when they left it to the award of Diarmaid, who pronounced the celebrated decision, *To every cow belongs its calf*," etc.

It is to be observed that the Annals both of Tighernach and Ulster attribute the success of the Northerns to St. Columba's intercession : *per orationem Coluim-cille dicentis*, etc., while the Four Masters, with their usual caution, merely state that *Colam cille do raidh*, " Colum-cille said," adding, from Tighernach, the verses which were supposed to have produced so marvellous a result.

Diarmait, who was now on the throne, was the head of the Southern branch of the Hy-Neill race ; and the chiefs of the two main sections of the Northern branch, namely, the Cinel Eoghain and Cinel Conaill, had already distinguished themselves by military enterprise, for in 543 the very same individuals won the battle of Sligo, and slew Eoghan Beul, king of Connaught; and again, in 549, the Cinel-Eoghain brothers slew Ailill Inbanna, the succeeding king of Connaught, at the battle of Cuil-Conaire in Carra, in the county of Mayo. They now espoused the cause of the Connacian chief, and it may be that some affront offered to their kinsman Columba, seconded by his instigation, produced the battle of Cul-Dreimhne, which, like that of Sligo, was fought on Connacian ground, but near the boundary between it and Ulster. The relation of the parties who engaged in this strife will be most readily understood from the following genealogical view :—

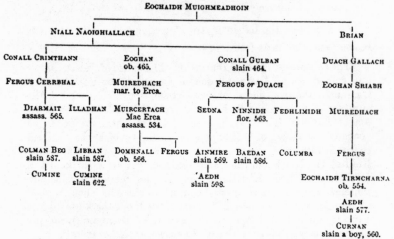

EOCHAIDH MUIGHMEADHOIN

NIALL NAOIGHIALLACH — BRIAN

CONALL CRIMTHANN | EOGHAN ob. 465. | CONALL GULBAN slain 464. | DUACH GALLACH

FERGUS CERRBHAL | MUIREDHACH mar. to Erca. | FERGUS or DUACH | EOGHAN SRIABH

DIARMAIT assass. 565. | ILLADHAN | MUIRCERTACH Mac Erca assass. 534. | SEDNA NINNIDH flor. 563. FEDHLIMIDH | MUIREDHACH

COLMAN BEG slain 587. | LIBRAN slain 587. | DOMHNALL FERGUS ob. 566. | AINMIRE slain 569. BAEDAN slain 586. COLUMBA | FERGUS

CUMINE | CUMINE slain 622. | AEDH slain 598. | EOCHAIDH TIRMCHARNA ob. 554.

AEDH slain 577.

CURNAN slain a boy, 560.

The promoter of this sanguinary contest became now, according to O'Donnell's authorities, the subject of ecclesiastical censure.

Thus we find St. Columba directly or indirectly concerned in three battles, the earliest of which occurred the year but one before his retirement to Britain, and the others at later periods, one of them after he had been twenty-four years in the abbacy of Hy. The first his biographers and panegyrists acknowledge to have been the grand error of his life, for which he paid the penalty of pilgrimage; but to save his character after he became the apostle of the Northern Picts, and the religious exemplar of the Albanian Scots, the device is resorted to of antedating the other occurrences in which the failing of his nature betrayed itself; and whereas his participation in these evils could not be denied, it was thrust back into the irresponsible part of his life, rather than allow it to be numbered among the acts of his maturity. That Columba, closely allied to the principals in these deeds of strife, and within one step himself of the object they were contending for, should look on with indifference, is not to be expected,—especially in an age of revolution, and among a people whose constitution and national construction rendered civil faction almost inseparable from their existence. It was not until 804, that the monastic communities of Ireland were formally exempted from military service; and the endeavours of Fothadh the Canonist, in procuring this enactment from Aedh Oirdnidhe, the monarch of Ireland, form the subject of panegyric and special mention in the Annals. That, even among themselves, the members of powerful communities were not insensible to the spirit of faction, appears from numerous entries in the ancient Annals. Of these, two—of which one relates to a Columbian house—may here be adduced as examples: A.D. 673, "A battle was fought at Argamoyn between the fraternities of Clonmacnois and Durrow, where Dermod Duff, son of Donnell, was killed, and Diglac, son of Dubliss, with 200 men of the fraternity of Durrow. Bresal, son of Murchadh, with the fraternity of Clonmacnois, was victor." A.D. 816, "A battle was fought by Cathal, son of Dunlang, and the fraternity of Tigh-Munna [Taghmon] against the fraternity of Ferns, in which 400 were slain. Maelduin, son of Cennfaeladh, abbot of Raphoe, of the fraternity of Colum-cille, was slain. The fraternity of Colum-cille went to Tara to curse [king] Aedh." The same principle which caused St. Columba's panegyrists to represent his battles as delinquencies of his *youth*, operated with the Four Masters, when compiling their comprehensive Annals from earlier authorities, in dealing with these oft-recurring monastic encounters, and as there was no opening for a transfer of the blame, they *suppressed* the mention of them.

THE LIFE OF SAINT COLUMBA.

IN THE NAME OF JESUS CHRIST.—THE PREFACE BEGINNETH.

In beginning, with the help of Christ, in compliance with the urgent requests of my brethren, to write the life of our blessed Patron, I shall take care to warn, in the first place, others who may read it, to believe the facts which it records, and to attend more to the matter than to the words, which, as I think, sound harsh and barbarous. Let them remember that the kingdom of God consisteth not in richness of eloquence, but in the blossoming of faith, and let them not for any names of men, or tribes, or obscure places in the base Scotic tongue, which, as I think, seem rude when compared with the various languages of foreign nations, despise a record of useful deeds wrought not without the help of God. We must also warn our readers that many other things regarding this man of blessed memory, well worthy of being told, have been omitted for the sake of brevity ; in order not to tire their patience, a few only out of many have been recorded here. And this, as I think, every person who reads the following work will perhaps observe, that of the great actions of the same holy man, popular fame has published the less important, when compared even with the few which we shall now briefly relate. From this point, in this our first brief preface, I now proceed, with the help of God, to explain in the commencement of the second, the name of our holy prelate.

IN THE NAME OF JESUS CHRIST.—THE SECOND PREFACE.

THERE was a man of venerable life and blessed memory, the father and founder of monasteries, having the same name as Jonah the prophet; for though its sound is different in the three different languages, yet its signification is the same in all: what in Hebrew is Iona, in the Greek language is called Περιστερὰ, and in the Latin Columba. Such and so great a name was not given, it is believed, to the man of God without a special providence. For according to the faith of the Gospels, the Holy Ghost is shown to have descended on the only begotten Son of the Eternal Father, in the form of that little bird called the dove; and hence for the most part in the sacred books the dove is known to designate in a mystical sense the Holy Ghost. Hence also our Saviour in His Gospel has ordered His disciples to preserve the simplicity of the dove ingrafted in a pure heart, for the dove is a simple and innocent bird. By that name, therefore, it was meet that the simple and innocent man should be called, who gave to the Holy Ghost a dwelling-place in himself by his dove-like ways; a name to which may with propriety be applied what is written in the Proverbs, " A good name is rather to be chosen than great riches." Justly, therefore, not only from the days of his infancy was our president, by the gift of God, honoured by this special name, but even many long years before his birth it was given to him as a child of the promise in a wonderful prophecy of a soldier of Christ to whom it was revealed by the Holy Ghost. For Maucta, a pilgrim from Britain, a holy man, a disciple of St. Patrick the Bishop, gave the following prophecy of our Patron, as is known by us on the testimony of learned ancients. " In the last ages of the world," he said, " a son shall be born, whose name Columba shall be announced in every province of the isles of the ocean, and brilliantly shall he enlighten the last ages of the earth. The little farms of his small monastery and of mine shall be divided by the boundary of a narrow fence, and he shall be a man most dear to God, and of great merit in His sight." In describing the life and character of our Columba, I shall in the first place, as briefly as I can, give a general summary, and place before my readers' eyes an image of his holy life. I also briefly shall notice some of his miracles, as a foretaste to those who eagerly read them, the more detailed account of which shall be given in the three last books. The first shall be his prophetical revelations—the second his divine virtues wrought by him—the third the apparitions of angels and some manifestations of the brightness of heaven upon the man of God. Let no one think of me as either stating what is not true regarding so great a man, or recording anything doubtful or uncertain. Let him know that I will tell with all candour, and without any ambiguity, what I have learned from the consistent narrative of my predecessors, trustworthy and discerning men, and that my narrative is founded either on written authorities anterior to my own times, or on what I have myself heard from some learned and faithful ancients, unhesitatingly attesting facts, the truth of which they had themselves diligently inquired into.

St. Columba then was born of noble parents; his father was Fedilmith, son of Fergus, and his mother was Aethne, whose father can be called in Latin Filius Navis, but in the Scotic tongue Mac Nave. In the second year after the battle of Culedrebina (fought A.D. 561), and in the forty-second of his age, St. Columba, resolving to seek a foreign country for the love of Christ, sailed from Scotia (Ireland) to Britain. From his boyhood he had been brought up in Christian training in the study of wisdom, and by the grace of God had so preserved the integrity of his body, and the purity of soul, that though dwelling on earth he appeared to live like the saints in heaven. For he was angelic in appearance, graceful in speech, holy in work, with talents of the highest order, and consummate prudence; he lived a soldier of Christ during thirty-four years in an island. He never could spend the space of even one hour without study, or prayer, or writing, or some other holy occupation. So incessantly was he engaged night and day in the unwearied exercise of fasting and watching, that the burden of each of these austerities would seem beyond the power of all human endurance. And still in all these he was beloved by all, for a holy joy ever beaming on his face revealed the joy and gladness with which the Holy Spirit filled his inmost soul.

BOOK I.

OF HIS PROPHETIC REVELATIONS.

CHAPTER I.

A brief narrative of his great Miracles.

ACCORDING to the promise given above, I shall commence this book with a brief account of the evidences which the venerable man gave of his power. By virtue of his prayer, and in the name of our Lord Jesus Christ, he healed several persons suffering under various diseases; and he alone, by the assistance of God, expelled from this our island, which now has the primacy, innumerable hosts of malignant spirits, whom he saw with his bodily eyes assailing himself, and beginning to bring deadly distempers on his monastic brotherhood. Partly by mortification, and partly by a bold resistance, he subdued, with the help of Christ, the furious rage of wild beasts. The surging waves, also, at times rolling mountains high in a great tempest, became quickly at his prayer quiet and smooth, and his ship, in which he then happened to be, reached the desired haven in a perfect calm.

When returning from the country of the Picts, where he had been for some days, he hoisted his sail when the breeze was against him to confound the Druids, and made as rapid a voyage as if the wind had been favourable. On other occasions, also, contrary winds were at his prayers changed into fair. In that same country, he took a white stone from the river, and blessed it for the working of certain cures; and that stone, contrary to nature, floated like an apple when placed in water. This divine miracle was wrought in the presence of King Brude and his household. In the same country, also, he performed a still greater miracle, by raising to life the dead child of an humble believer, and restoring him in life and vigour to his father and mother. At another time, while the blessed man was yet a young deacon in Hibernia, residing with the holy bishop Findbarr, the wine required for the sacred mysteries failed, and he changed by his prayer pure water into true wine. An immense blaze of heavenly light was on many and wholly distinct occasions seen by some of the brethren to surround him in the light of day, as well as in the darkness of the night. He was also favoured with the sweet and most delightful society of bright hosts of the holy angels. He often saw, by the revelation of the Holy Ghost, the souls of some just men carried by angels to the highest heavens. And the reprobates too he very frequently beheld carried to hell by demons. He very often foretold the future deserts, sometimes joyful, and sometimes sad, of many persons while they were still living in mortal flesh. In the dreadful crash of wars he obtained from God, by the virtue of prayer, that some kings should be conquered, and others come off victorious. And such a grace as this he enjoyed, not only while alive in this world, but even after his departure from the flesh, as God, from whom all the saints derive their honour, has made him still a victorious and most valiant champion in battle. I shall give one example of especial honour conferred by Almighty God on this honourable man, the event having occurred the day before the Saxon prince Oswald went forth to fight with Catlon (Ceadualla of Bede), a very valiant king of the Britons. For as this same King Oswald, after pitching his camp, in readiness for the battle, was sleeping one day on a pillow in his tent, he saw St. Columba in a vision, beaming with angelic brightness, and of figure so majestic that his head seemed to touch the clouds. The blessed man having announced his name to the king, stood in the midst of the camp, and covered it all with his brilliant garment, except at one small distant point; and at the same time he uttered those cheering words which the Lord spake to Jesua Ben Nun before the passage of the Jordan, after Moses' death, saying, "Be strong and of a good courage; behold, I shall be with thee," etc. Then St. Columba having said these words to the king in the vision, added, "March out this following night from your camp to battle, for on this occasion the Lord has granted to me that your foes shall be put to flight, that your enemy Catlon shall be delivered into your hands, and that after the battle you shall return in triumph, and have a happy reign." The king, awaking at these words, assembled his council and related the vision, at which they were all encouraged; and so the whole people promised that, after their return from the war, they would believe and be baptized, for up to that time all that Saxon land had been wrapt in the darkness of paganism and ignorance, with the exception of King Oswald and the twelve men who had been baptized with him during his exile among the Scots. What more need I say? On the very next night, King Oswald, as he had been directed in the vision, went forth from his camp to battle, and had a much smaller army than the numerous hosts opposed to him, yet he obtained from the Lord, according to His promise, an easy and decisive victory—for King Catlon was slain, and the conqueror, on his return after the battle, was ever after established by God as the Bretwalda of all Britain. I, Adamnan, had this narrative from the lips of my predecessor, the Abbot Failbe, who solemnly declared that he had himself heard King Oswald relating this same vision to Segine the abbot.

But another fact must not be omitted, that by some poems composed in the Scotic language in praise of the same blessed man, and by the commemoration of his name, certain wicked men of lewd conversation, and men of blood, were saved from the hands of their enemies, who in the night had surrounded the house in which they were singing these hymns. They safely escaped through the flames, the swords, and the spears; and, strange to tell, a few of those only who despised these commemorations of the holy man, and refused to join in the hymns, perished in that assault of the enemy. It is not two or three witnesses, as the law requires, but even hundreds and more, that could be cited in proof of this miracle. Nor is it in one place or on one occasion only that the same is known to have happened, but even at different times and places, in both Scotia (Ireland) and Britain, it is proved beyond all doubt that the like security was obtained, in the same manner and by the same means. I have learned this for certain, from well-informed men in those very countries where similar miracles have taken place.

But, to return to the point in hand: among the miracles which this same man of the Lord, while dwelling in mortal flesh, performed by the gift of God, was his foretelling the future by the spirit of prophecy, with which he was highly favoured from his early years, and making known to those who were present what was happening in other places: for though absent in body he was present in spirit, and could look on things that were widely apart, according to the words of St. Paul, "He that is joined unto the Lord is one spirit."

Hence this same man of the Lord, St. Columba, when a few of the brethren would sometimes inquire into the matter, did not deny but that by some divine intuition, and through a wonderful expansion of his inner soul, he beheld the whole universe drawn together and laid open to his sight, as in one ray of the sun.

This account of the miracles of the holy man I have given here for this purpose, that my reader, in this brief sketch, may have a foretaste of the richer banquet which is before him, in the fuller narrative which is to be given, with the assistance of the Lord, in the three following books.   Here it appears to me not improper, though it may be out of the usual order, to record some prophecies which the blessed man gave at different times, regarding certain holy and illustrious men.

CHAPTER II.

Of St. Finten the Abbot, son of Tailchan.

ST. FINTEN, who was afterwards very well known throughout all the churches of the Scots, having, by the grace of God, preserved from his boyhood purity of body and soul, and being devoted to the study of divine wisdom, had nourished from his youthful years this one resolve in his heart, that he would leave Hibernia and go abroad to St. Columba.   Burning with that desire, he went to an old friend, the most prudent and venerable cleric in his country, who was called in the Scotic tongue Columb Crag, to get some sound advice from him.   When he had laid open his mind to him, he received the following answer: " As thy devout wish is, I feel, inspired by God, who can presume to say that thou shouldest not cross the sea to St. Columba ?"   At the same moment two monks of St. Columba happened to arrive, and when they were asked about their journey, they replied: "We have lately come across from Britain, and to-day we have come from the Oakwood of Calgach (Daire Calgaich, or Derry).   "Is he well," says Columb Crag, " your holy father Columba?"   Then they burst into tears, and answered with great sorrow, " Our patron is indeed well, for a few days ago he departed to Christ."   Hearing this, Finten and Columb, and all who were there present, fell on their faces on the ground, and wept bitterly.   Finten then asked, " Whom did he leave as his successor ?"   " Baithene, his disciple," they replied.   And as all cried out, "·It is meet and right," Columba said to Finten, " What wilt thou now do, Finten ?"   He answered, " With God's permission, I will sail over to Baithene, that wise and holy man, and if he receive me I will take him as my abbot."   Then kissing the forementioned Columb, and bidding him farewell, he prepared for his voyage, and setting sail without the least delay, arrived at the Iouan island (Hy, now corruptly Iona). As up to that time his name was wholly unknown in those places, he was only received at first with the hospitality given to every unknown stranger; but next day he sent a messenger to Baithene, and asked to have a personal interview. Baithene, ever kind and affable to strangers, ordered him to be introduced. Being at once brought in, he first, as seemed meet, knelt down upon the ground; and then being ordered by the holy abbot to rise and be seated, he was asked by Baithene, who as yet knew nothing of his family, province, name, or life, what was his motive for encountering the labour of the voyage. In reply to the inquiry thus made he told everything in order, and then humbly asked to be admitted. The holy abbot, hearing these things from his guest, and recognising him at the same time as the man of whom St. Columba had some time previously made a prophecy, replied : "Truly, my son, I ought to give thanks to my God for thy arrival, but be thou assured of this, that thou wilt not be one of our monks." On hearing this the stranger was very much grieved, and said : "Perhaps I am unworthy to become thy monk." "It is not because thou art unworthy, as thou sayest, that I gave that answer," immediately replied the abbot, "for I would indeed prefer retaining you with me, but I cannot disobey the command of St. Columba, my predecessor, by whom the Holy Ghost prophesied of thee. For, as I was alone with him one day, among other things which he foretold was the following : 'Hearken very attentively, O Baithene,' said he, 'to these my words, for shortly after my welcome and earnestly longed-for departure from this world to Christ, a certain brother from Scotia (Ireland), named Finten, son of Tailchan, of the tribe Mocumoie, who is now carefully guarding his youthful years with a good life, and is very well versed in sacred studies, will, I say, come to thee, and humbly ask thee to receive and enrol him with your other monks. But this has not been appointed for him in the foreknowledge of God, that he should become the monk of any abbot, for he has long since been chosen of God to be an abbot of monks and a leader of souls to the kingdom of heaven. Thou shalt not therefore detain that illustrious man with thee on these islands of ours, lest thou shouldst even seem to oppose the will of God, but thou shalt make known to him what I have told thee, and send him back in peace to Scotia (Ireland), that he may found a monastery in the parts of the Leinstermen, near the sea, and that there feeding the flock of Christ, he shall lead a countless host of souls to their heavenly country.'" The holy youth hearing this burst into tears, and returning thanks to Christ, said: "Be it unto me according to

the prophecy and wonderful foreknowledge of St. Columba."
At the same time, in obedience to the words of the saints, he
received the blessing of Baithene, and sailed back in peace to
Scotia (Ireland).

I have heard this as an undoubted fact from the lips of an
aged and pious priest and soldier of Christ, called Oissene, son
of Ernan, of the tribe Mocu Neth Corb, who averred that he had
himself heard these very words from the lips of St. Finten, son
of Tailchan, whose monk he himself had been.

CHAPTER III.

Prophecy of St. Columba regarding Ernene, son of Crasen.

On another occasion, while the blessed man was residing for
a few months in the midland part of Hibernia, when founding
by divine inspiration his monastery, which in the Scotic tongue
is called Dair-mag (Durrow), was pleased to pay a visit to the
brethren who dwelt in St. Ceran's monastery, Clon (Clonmac-
noise). As soon as it was known that he was near, all flocked
from their little grange farms near the monastery, and, along
with those who were within it, ranged themselves, with enthu-
siasm, under the abbot Alither ; then advancing beyond the
enclosure of the monastery, they went out as one man to
meet St. Columba, as if he were an angel of the Lord.
Humbly bowing down, with their faces to the ground, in his
presence, they kissed him most reverently, and singing hymns
of praise as they went they conducted him with all honour
to the Church. Over the saint, as he walked, a canopy made
of wood was supported by four men walking by his side, lest
the holy abbot, St. Columba, should be troubled by the crowd
of brethren pressing upon him. At that very time, a boy
attached to the monastery, who was mean in dress and look,
and hitherto had not stood well in the opinions of the
seniors, concealing himself as well as he could, came forward
stealthily, that he might touch unperceived even the hem of the
cloak which the blessed man wore, without his feeling or knowing it. This, however, did not escape the saint, for he knew
with the eyes of his soul what he could not see taking place
behind him with the eyes of his body. Stopping therefore
suddenly, and putting out his hand behind him, he seized the
boy by the neck, and bringing him round set him before his
face. The crowd of bystanders cried out : " Let him go, let
him go : why do you touch that unfortunate and naughty

boy?" But the saint solemnly uttered these prophetic words from his pure heart: "Suffer it to be so now, brethren;" then turning to the boy, who was in the greatest terror, he said, "My son, open thy mouth, and put out thy tongue." The boy did as he was bid, and in great alarm opened his mouth and put out his tongue: the saint extended to it his holy hand, and after carefully blessing it pronounced his prophecy in the following words: "Though this boy appears to you now very contemptible and worthless, let no one on that account despise him. For from this hour, not only will he not displease you, but he will give you every satisfaction; from day to day he shall advance by degrees in good conduct, and in the virtues of the soul; from this day, wisdom and prudence shall be more and more increased in him, and great shall be his progress in this your community: his tongue also shall receive from God the gift of both wholesome doctrine and eloquence." This was Ernene, son of Crasen, who was afterwards famous and most highly honoured in all the churches of Scotia (Ireland). He himself told all these words which were prophesied regarding himself, as written above, to the abbot Segine, in the attentive hearing of my predecessor Failbe, who was present at the time with Segine, and from whose lips I myself have come to know all that I have stated. But during this short time that the saint was a guest in the monastery of Clon, there were many other things also which he prophesied by the revelation of the Holy Ghost; as, for instance, about the discord which arose a long time after among the churches of Scotia (Ireland), on account of the difference with regard to the Easter Feast; and about some visits of angels distinctly made to himself, certain places within the enclosure of the monastery being at that time thus resorted to by the angels.

CHAPTER IV.

Of the arrival of St. Cainnech, the Abbot, who had been previously announced in prophecy by St. Columba.

AT another time, in the Iouan island (Hy, now Iona), on a day when the tempest was fierce and the sea was exceedingly boisterous, the saint, as he sat in the house, gave orders to his brethren, saying, "Prepare the guest-chamber quickly, and draw water to wash the strangers' feet." One of the brethren upon this inquired: "Who can cross the Sound safely, narrow though it be, on so perilous and stormy a day?" The saint, on hearing this, thus made answer, "The Almighty has given a calm even in this tempest to a certain holy and excellent man, who will arrive here among us before evening." And lo ! the same day, the ship for which the brethren had some time been looking out arrived, according to the saint's prediction, and brought St. Cainnech. The saint went forth with the brethren to meet him and received him with all honour and hospitality. But the sailors who had been with St. Cainnech, when they were asked by the brethren what sort of a voyage they had had, told them, even as St. Columba had predicted, about both the tempest and the calm which God had given in the same sea and at the same time, with an amazing distinction between the two. The tempest they saw at a distance, yet they said they did not feel it.

CHAPTER V.

Of the Danger to the holy Bishop Colman Mocusailni in the Sea, near the island called Rechru.

ON another day, also, while St. Columba was engaged in his mother-church, he suddenly cried out, with a smile, "Columbanus, the son of Beogna, has just now set out on a voyage to us, and is in great danger in the rolling tides of Brecan's whirlpool: he is sitting at the prow and raising both his hands to heaven: he is also blessing that angry and dreadful sea: yet in this the Lord only frightens him, for the ship in which he is shall not be wrecked in the storm; but this is rather to excite him to pray more fervently, that by God's favour he may escape the danger of his voyage, and reach us in safety.

CHAPTER VI.

Of Cormac.

ON another occasion also St. Columba prophesied in the following manner of Cormac, grandson of Lethan, a truly pious man, who not less than three times went in search of a desert in the ocean, but did not find it. " In his desire to find a desert, Cormac is this day, for the second time, now embarking from that district which lies at the other side of the river Moda (the Moy, in Sligo), and is called Eirros Domno (Erris, in Mayo); nor even this time shall he find what he seeks, and that for no other fault than that he has irregularly allowed to accompany him in the voyage a monk who is going away from his own proper abbot without obtaining his consent."

CHAPTER VII.

Prophecy of the blessed man regarding the Tumults of Battles fought at a distance.

ABOUT two years, as we have been told, after the battle of Cule-Drebene (in Connaught), at which time the blessed man first set sail and took his departure from Scotia (Ireland), it happened that on the very day and at the same hour when the battle, called in Scotic Ondemone (near Coleraine), was fought in Scotia (Ireland), the same man of God was then living in Britain with King Connall, the son of Comgell, and told him everything, as well about the battle itself, as also about those kings to whom the Lord granted the victory over their enemies. These kings were known as Ainmore, son of Setna, and the two sons of Mac Erca, Domnall and Forcus. And the saint, in like manner, prophesied of the king of the Cruithne, who was called Echoid Laib, and how, after being defeated, he escaped riding in his chariot.

On the Battle of the Miathi.

AT another time, after the lapse of many years from the above-mentioned battle, and while the holy man was in the Iouan island (Hy, now Iona), he suddenly said to his minister, Diormit, "Ring the bell." The brethren, startled at the sound, proceeded quickly to the church, with the holy prelate himself at their head. There he began, on bended knees, to say to them, "Let us pray now earnestly to the Lord for this people and King Aidan, for they are engaging in battle at this moment." Then after a short time he went out of the oratory, and, looking up to heaven, said, "The barbarians are fleeing now, and to Aidan is given the victory—a sad one though it be." And the blessed man in his prophecy declared the number of the slain in Aidan's army to be three hundred and three men.

CHAPTER VIII.

Prophecy of St. Columba regarding the Sons of King Aidan.

At another time, before the above-mentioned battle, the saint asked King Aidan about his successor to the crown. The king answered that of his three sons, Artur, Eochoid Find, and Domingart, he knew not which would have the kingdom after him. Then at once the saint prophesied on this wise, "None of

these three shall be king, for they shall fall in battle, slain by
their enemies; but now if thou hast any younger sons, let them
come to me, and that one of them whom the Lord has chosen to
be king will at once rush into my lap." When they were called
in, Eochoid Buide, according to the word of the saint, advanced
and rested in his bosom. Immediately the saint kissed him,
and, giving him his blessing, said to his father, " This one shall
survive and reign as king after thee, and his sons shall reign
after him." And so were all these things fully accomplished
afterwards in their time. For Artur and Eochoid Find were
not long after killed in the above-mentioned battle of the
Miathi; Domingart was also defeated and slain in battle in
Saxonia; while Eochoid Buide succeeded his father on the
throne.

Of Domnall, son of Aid.

DOMNALL, son of Aid, while yet a boy, was brought by those
who brought him up to St. Columba on the ridge of Ceatt
(Druim Ceatt in Londonderry), who looked at him and inquired,
" Whose son is this whom you have brought here?" They
answered, " This is Domnall, son of Aid, who is brought to
thee for this purpose, that he may return enriched by thy
blessing." The saint blessed him immediately, and said, " He
shall survive all his brethren, and be a very famous king, nor
shall he be ever delivered into the hands of his enemies; but
in his old age, in his own house, and with a crowd of his
familiar friends around him, he shall die peacefully in his bed."
All this was truly fulfilled in him, as the blessed man had
foretold.

Of Scandlan, son of Colman.

AT the same time and place, the saint, wishing to visit
Scandlan, son of Colman, went to him where he was kept in
prison by King Aid, and when he had blessed him he comforted
him, saying, " Son, do not distress yourself, but rather rejoice
and take courage, for King Aid, who has you a prisoner, will go
out of this world before you, and after some time of exile you
shall reign in your own nation for thirty years. And again
you shall be driven from your kingdom, and be in exile for
some days; but after that you shall be called home again by
your people, and shall reign for three short terms." All this
was fully accomplished according to the prediction of the saint.
For in thirty years he had to leave his throne, and continued
in exile for some time; and then being recalled by his people,

he reigned not three years, as he expected, but three months, and at the end of that time he died.

A Prophecy of the blessed man regarding two other Kings, who were called the two grandsons of Muiredach—Baitan, son of Maic Erc, and Eochoid, son of Domnall.

AT another time, while travelling through the rough and rocky country which is called Artdamuirchol (Ardnamurchan), he heard his companions—Laisran, son of Feradach, and Diormit, his minister—speaking on the way of the two above-named kings, and addressed them in these words, "O my dear children, why do you talk thus foolishly of these men? Both of these kings of whom you are now conversing are newly slain, and have had their heads cut off by their enemies. And this very day some sailors shall come here from Scotia (Ireland), and tell you the same about these kings." That same day some sailors arrived from Hibernia, at a place which is called Muirbolc Paradisi (Portnamurloch in Lismore), and told the two above-named companions, who were now sailing in the same ship with the saint, how these kings had been slain, and thus the prophecy of the venerable man fulfilled.

Prophecy of the holy man regarding Oingus, son of Aid Comman.

WHEN he and his two brothers were driven from his country, he came as an exile to the saint, who was then wandering in Britain, and who, in blessing him, uttered these prophetic words from his holy heart, "This youth shall survive when his other brothers are gone, and he shall reign a long time in his native country; his enemies shall fall before him, while he shall never fall into their hands, but in old age he shall die peacefully in the midst of his friends." All this was fully accomplished according to the saint's words. This was Oingus, surnamed Bronbachal.

Prophecy of the blessed man regarding the son of King Dermit, who in the Scotic language is called Aid Slane.

ON another occasion, when the blessed man was sojourning for some days in Scotia (Ireland), he spoke in the following prophetic strain to the above-mentioned Aid, who had come to visit him: —"Thou must take care, my son, lest, for the sin of murdering thy kinsman, thou lose the right of governing the whole of

Hibernia, as was first assigned thee by God; for if at any time thou dost commit that sin, thou shalt not hold the whole of thy father's kingdom, but only a part of it in thine own tribe, and that but for a short time." These words of the saint were on this wise fulfilled according to the prediction, that after Aid had treacherously killed Suibne, son of Columban, he reigned, it is said, no longer than four years and three months, and that only as colleague in the kingdom.

Prophecy of the blessed man regarding King Roderc, son of Tothal, who reigned on the Rock of Cluaith (Alcluith or Dumbarton).

THIS same king being on friendly terms with the holy man, sent to him on one occasion a secret message by Lugbe Mocumin, as he was anxious to know whether he would be killed by his enemies or not. But when Lugbe was being closely inquired at by the saint regarding the king, his kingdom, and people, he answered in a tone of pity, "Why do you ask about that wretched man, who is quite unable to tell at what hour he may be killed by his enemies?" Then the saint replied, "He shall never be delivered into the hands of his enemies; he will die at home on his own pillow." And the prophecy of the saint regarding King Roderc was fully accomplished; for, according to his word, he died quietly in his own house.

CHAPTER IX.

Prophecy of the Saint regarding two boys, one of whom, according to the Saint's word, died at the end of a week.

ON another occasion, two men of low rank in life came to the saint, who was then in the Iouan island (Hy, now Iona). One of them, named Meldan, brought his son to the saint and asked him what kind of future he would enjoy. To whom the saint replied, "Is not this the Sabbath day? Thy son will die on the sixth day at the end of next week, and will be buried here on the eighth day, that is the Sabbath." Then the other man, named Glasderc, also took his son along with him, and venturing to make a similar inquiry, received the following answer from the saint, "Thy son Ernan will see his grand-children, and be buried in old age in this island." All this was fully accomplished in its own time, regarding the two boys, according to the words of the saint.

CHAPTER X.

Prophecy of the Saint regarding Colca, son of Aid Draignich, sprung from the grandsons of Fechureg, and regarding some secret sin of his mother.

THIS Colca residing one time in the Iouan island (Hy, now Iona) with the saint, was asked by him concerning his mother whether she was a pious woman or not. Colca answered him, " I have always known my mother to be good, and to bear that character." The saint then spoke these prophetic words: "Set out now at once for Scotia (Ireland), with God's help, and question thy mother closely regarding her very grievous secret sin, which she will not confess to any man." To carry out the advice thus given him he departed to Hibernia: and when he interrogated his mother closely, she at first denied, and then she at last confessed her sin. When she had done penance according to the judgment of the saint, she was absolved, wondering very much all the while at what was made known to the saint regarding her.

CHAPTER XI.

COLCA, however, returned to the saint, and remained with him for some days, and then asking about the end of his own days, received this answer from the saint:—"In thine own beloved country thou shalt be head of a church for many years, and when at any time thou happenest to see thy butler making merry with a company of his friends at supper, and twirling the ladle round in the strainer, know that then in a short time thou shalt die." What more need I say? This same prophecy of the blessed man was exactly fulfilled, as it was foretold to Colca.

CHAPTER XII.

Regarding Laisrean, the gardener, a holy man.

ON a certain day, the holy man ordered one of his monks named Trena, of the tribe Mocuruntir, to go a message for him to Scotia (Ireland). While he was preparing the ship in haste to obey the orders of the man of God, he complained before the saint that one of the sailors was wanting. The saint immediately answered him, and uttered these words from his sacred

breast, " The sailor who is, thou sayest, absent, I cannot just
now find.   But go in peace; thou shalt have a favourable and
steady breeze till thou reach Hibernia.   Thou shalt see a man
coming to meet thee from a distance, and he will be the first to
seize the prow of thy ship in Scotia (Ireland); he shall be with
thee during the time of thy sojourn in Hibernia, and accompany
thee on thy return to us, as a man chosen by God, who in this
very monastery of mine will live piously the remainder of his
days."   What more can I add ?   Trena received the saint's
blessing, and crossed over at full sail during the whole voyage,
and lo ! as his little ship was nearing the port, Laisran Mocumoie ran forward before the others and caught the prow.   The
sailors knew that this was the very man of whom the saint had
spoken beforehand.

CHAPTER XIII.

How the Saint knew and told beforehand about a great Whale.

ONE day when the venerable man was staying in the Iouan
island (Hy, now Iona), a certain brother named Berach intended
to sail to the Ethican island (Tiree), and going to the saint in the
morning asked his blessing.   The saint looking at him, said,
" O my son, take very great care this day not to attempt sailing
direct over the open sea to the Ethican land (Tiree); but rather
take a circuit, and sail round by the smaller islands, for this
reason, that thou be not thrown into great terror by a huge
monster, and hardly be able to escape."   On receiving the
saint's blessing he departed, and when he reached his ship, he
set sail without giving heed to the saint's words.   But as he
was crossing over the larger arms of the Ethican sea, he and
the sailors who were with him looked out, and lo, a whale, of
huge and amazing size, raised itself like a mountain, and as it
floated on the surface, it opened its mouth, which, as it gaped,
was bristling with teeth.   Then the rowers, hauling in their
sail, pulled back in the utmost terror, and had a very narrow
escape from the agitation of the waves caused by the motion of
the monster; and they were also struck with wonder as they
remembered the prophetic words of the saint.   On the morning
of that same day, as Baithene was going to sail to the forenamed
island, the saint told him about this whale, saying, " Last night,
at midnight, a great whale rose from the depth of the sea, and it
will float this day on the surface of the ocean between the Iouan
and Ethican islands (Iona and Tiree)."   Baithene answered and
said, " That beast and I are under the power of God."   " Go in

peace,"- said the saint; "thy faith in Christ shall defend thee from this danger." Baithene accordingly, having received the saint's blessing, sailed from the harbour; and after they had sailed a considerable distance, he and his companions saw the whale; and while all the others were much terrified, he alone was without fear, and raising up both his hands, blessed the sea and the whale. At the same moment the enormous brute plunged down under the waves, and never afterwards appeared to them.

CHAPTER XIV.

Prophecy of the holy man regarding a certain Baitan, who with others sailed in search of a desert in the ocean.

AT another time, a certain man named Baitan, by race a descendant of Niath Taloirc, when setting out with others to seek a desert in the sea, asked the saint's blessing. The saint bidding him adieu uttered this prophecy regarding him : "This man who is going in search of a desert in the ocean shall not be buried in the desert, but in that place where a woman shall drive sheep over his grave." The same Baitan, after long wanderings on stormy seas, returned to his native country without finding the desert, and remained for many years the head of a small monastic house, which is called in the Scotic tongue Lathreginden (not identified). When after a while he died and was buried, in the Oakgrove of Galgach (Derry), it happened at the same time that on account of some hostile inroad the poor people with their wives and children fled for sanctuary to the church of that place. Whence it occurred that on a certain day a woman was caught, as she was driving her lambs over the grave of this same man who was newly buried. Then a holy priest who was present and saw this, said, " Now is fulfilled the prophecy which St. Columba uttered many years ago." And this I myself was told regarding Baitan, by that same priest and soldier of Christ, Mailodran by name, of the tribe of Mocurin.

CHAPTER XV.

Prophecy of the holy man regarding a certain Neman, who was not a real penitent.

AT another time, the saint came to the Hinbina island (Eilean-na-naoimh, one of the Garveloch islands), and that same day he gave orders that even the penitents should enjoy some indulgence in respect of their food. Now there

was among the penitents in that place a certain Neman, son
of Cathair, who, though ordered by the saint, declined to accept
the offer of this little indulgence. Him then the saint addressed
in these words: "O Neman, art thou not accepting some
indulgence in food as it is kindly granted by me and Baitan?
The time shall come when thou wilt be stealthily eating mare's
flesh, as thou liest concealed in the woods with robbers." And
accordingly that same man afterwards returned to the world,
and was found in a forest with robbers taking and eating off a
wooden griddle such flesh as the saint had foretold.

CHAPTER XVI.

Regarding a certain unhappy man who lay with his Mother.

AT another time, the saint called out the brethren at the
dead of night, and when they were assembled in the church
said to them: "Now let us pray fervently to the Lord, for at
this hour a sin unheard of in the world has been committed,
for, which rigorous vengeance that is justly due is very much
to be feared." Next day he spoke of this sin to a few who
were asking him about it. "After a few months," he said,
" that unhappy wretch will come here to the Iouan island (Hy,
now Iona) with Lugaid, who is unaware of the sin." Accordingly after the few months had passed away, the saint one day
spoke to Diormit, and ordered him, " Rise quickly; lo! Lugaid
is coming. Tell him to send off the wretch whom he has with
him in the ship to the Malean island (Mull), that he may not
tread the sod of this island." He went to the sea in obedience
to the saint's injunction, and told Lugaid as he was approaching
all the words of the saint regarding the unhappy man. On hearing the directions, that unhappy man vowed that he would never
eat food with others until he had seen St. Columba and spoken
to him. Diormit therefore returned to the saint, and told him
the words of the poor wretch. The saint, on hearing them, went
down to the haven, and as Baitan was citing the authority of
Holy Scriptures, and suggesting that the repentance of the unhappy man should be received, the saint immediately replied to
him, "O Baitan! this man has committed fratricide like Cain, and
become an adulterer with his mother." Then the poor wretch,
casting himself upon his knees on the beach, promised that he
would comply with all the rules of penance, according to the
judgment of the saint. The saint said to him, "If thou do
penance in tears and lamentations for twelve years among the
Britons, and never to the day of thy death return to Scotia (Ire-

land), perhaps God may pardon thy sin." Having said these words, the saint turned to his own friends and said, "This man is a son of perdition, who will not perform the penance he has promised, but will soon return to Scotia (Ireland), and there in a short time be killed by his enemies." All this happened exactly according to the saint's prophecy; for the wretched man, returning to Hibernia about the same time, fell into the hands of his enemies in the region called Lea (Firli, in Ulster), and was murdered. He was of the descendants of Turtre.

CHAPTER XVII.

Of the Vowel I.

ONE day Baithene came to the saint and said, "I want some one of the brethren to look over with me and correct the psalter which I have written." Hearing this, the saint said, "Why give us this trouble without any cause? In that psalter of thine, of which thou speakest, there is not one superfluous letter to be found, nor is any wanting except the one vowel I." And accordingly, when the whole psalter was read over, what the saint had said was found to be true.

CHAPTER XVIII.

Of the Book which fell into the Water-vessel, as the Saint had foretold.

IN the same way, on another day, as he was sitting by the hearth in the monastery, he saw at some distance Lugbe, of the tribe Mocumin, reading a book, and suddenly said to him, "Take care, my son, take care, for I think that the book thou readest is about to fall into a vessel full of water." And so it soon happened, for when the same youth rose soon after to perform some duty in the monastery, he forgot the word of the blessed man, and the book which he held negligently under his arm suddenly fell into the water-pot, which was full of water.

CHAPTER XIX.

Of the Inkhorn, awkwardly spilled.

ON another day a shout was given on the other side of the Sound of the Iouan island (Sound of Iona); the saint hearing the shout, as he was sitting in his little hut, which was made of planks, said, "The man who is shouting beyond the Sound is not of very sharp wit, for when he is here to-day he will upset my inkhorn and spill the ink.   Diormit, his minister, hearing this, stood a little in front of the door, and waited for the arrival of this troublesome guest, in order to save the inkhorn.   But for some cause or other he had soon to leave his place, and after his departure the unwelcome guest arrived; in his eager haste to kiss the saint, he upset the inkhorn with the hem of his garment and spilled the ink.

CHAPTER XX.

Of the arrival of another Guest foretold by the Saint.

So again at another time the saint spoke thus to his brethren on the third day of the week, " We intend to fast to-morrow, being Wednesday : and yet by the arrival of a certain troublesome guest the usual fast will be broken."   And so it happened as had been shown to the saint beforehand; for on the morning of that same Wednesday, another stranger was heard signalling across the Sound.   This was Aidan, the son of Fergno, who, it is said, was minister for twelve years to Brendan Mocualti. He was a very religious man, and his arrival, as the saint had foretold, broke the fast of that day.

CHAPTER XXI.

Of another man in distress who was crying across the same Sound.

ON another day the saint heard some person shouting across the Sound, and spoke on this wise, "That man who is shouting is much to be pitied, for he is coming here to us to ask some cure for the disease of his body; but it were better for him this day to do true penance for his sins, for at the close of this week he shall die."   These words those who were present told to the unhappy man when he arrived.   But he gave no heed to them when he had received what he asked, and quickly departed, yet before the end of the same week he died, according to the prediction of the saint.

CHAPTER XXII.

The Prophecy of the holy man regarding the Roman city, burnt by a sulphurous fire which fell from heaven.

ANOTHER time also, Lugbe, of the tribe Mocumin, of whom I spoke already, came to the saint one day after the grinding of the corn, but the saint's countenance shone with such wonderful brilliancy that he could not look upon it, and quickly fled in great terror. The saint gently clapped his hands and called him back; then on his return the saint asked him why he fled so quickly. " I fled," he replied, " because I was very much alarmed." Then becoming more confident, after a while, he ventured to ask the saint, " Hath any awful vision been shown to thee just now ? " The saint answered, " A very fearful vengeance hath just now been exacted in a distant corner of the world." " What vengeance ? " says the youth, " and where hath it taken place ? " The saint then addressed him thus : " A sulphurous fire hath been poured down from heaven this moment on a city which is subject to Rome, and within the Italian territory, and about three thousand men, besides women and children, have perished. Before the end of this year Gallican sailors shall come here from the provinces of Gaul, and tell thee these same things." His words proved true in a few months ; for the same Lugbe, happening to accompany the saint to the Head of the land (Kintyre), inquired at the captain and crew of a bark that had just arrived, and received from them all the news regarding the city and its inhabitants, exactly as it was foretold by the illustrious man.

CHAPTER XXIII.

The Vision of the blessed man regarding Laisran, son of Feradach.

ONE very cold day in winter the saint was much afflicted, and wept bitterly. His attendant, Diormit, asked the cause of his sadness, and received this answer from him, " With just reason am I sad to-day, my little child, seeing that my monks, now wearied after their severe labours, are engaged by Laisran in building a large house ; with this I am very much displeased." Strange to say, at that very moment, Laisran, who was living at the time in the monastery of the Oakwood Plain (Derry), felt somehow impelled, and as it were consumed by a fire within him, so that he commanded the monks to stop from working, and some refreshments to be made ready for them. He also gave directions that they were to rest not only that day, but also on other occasions of severe weather. The saint, hearing in spirit these words of consolation addressed by Laisran to his brethren, ceased weeping, and though he himself was living in the Iouan island (Hy, now Iona), he rejoiced with exceeding great joy, and told all the circumstances to his brethren, while at the same time he blessed Laisran for his timely relief to the monks.

CHAPTER XXIV.

How Feachna the Wise came as a Penitent to St. Columba, as he had foretold.

ANOTHER time the saint was sitting on the top of the mountain which overhangs this our monastery, at some distance from it, and turning to his attendant Diormit, said to him, " I am surprised that a certain ship from Scotia (Ireland) does not appear sooner: there is on board a certain wise man who has fallen into a great crime, but who, with tears of repentance, shall soon arrive." Not long after the attendant, looking to the south, saw the sail of a ship that was approaching the harbour. When its arrival was pointed out to the saint he got up quickly and said, " Let us go to meet this stranger, whose sincere penance is accepted by Christ." As soon as Feachna came on shore, he ran to meet the saint, who was coming down to the shore, and falling on his knees before him lamented most bitterly with wailing and tears, and there in the presence of all made open confession of his sins. Then the saint, also shedding tears, said to him, " Arise, my son, and be comforted ; the sins thou hast committed are forgiven thee, because, as it is written, ' a humble and contrite heart God doth not despise.' " He then arose, and the saint received him with great joy. After a few days he was sent to Baithene, who at that time was the superior of the monastery in the plain of Lunge (Maigh Lunge, in Tiree), and he journeyed thither in peace.

CHAPTER XXV.

The Prophecy of the holy man regarding his monk Cailtan.

AT another time he sent two of his monks to another of them named Cailtan, who was then superior in the cell which is called to this day after his brother Diuni, and is situated near the lake of the river Aba (Lochawe). The saint gave them the following instructions, " Run quickly to Cailtan, and tell him to come to me without delay." In obedience to the saint's command they went to the cell of Diuni, and told Cailtan the object of their mission. At once, and without the least delay, he set out along with the messengers of the saint, and soon reached his abode in the Iouan island (Hy, now Iona). On making his appearance he was addressed by the saint, "O Cailtan, thou hast done well by coming hither quickly in obedience to my summons ; rest now for a while. I sent for you to come to me for this reason, that, loving thee as a friend, I would wish thee to end thy days with me here in true obedience. For before the close of this week thou shalt depart in peace to the Lord." When he heard these words he gave thanks to God, embraced the saint with tears, and receiving his blessing, retired to the guest-chamber. He fell sick that same night, and passed away to Christ the Lord during that very week, as the saint had said.

CHAPTER XXVI.

The Foresight and Prophecy of the Saint regarding the two brothers who were Strangers.

ONE Lord's day a loud cry was heard beyond the above-mentioned Sound of which I speak so often. As soon as the saint heard it, he said to the brethren who were then with him, " Go directly and bring here before us at once the strangers that have now arrived from a distant land." They went accordingly and ferried the strangers across. The saint, after embracing them, asked them at once the object of their journey. In reply they said, " We are come to reside with thee for this year." The saint replied, " With me, as you say, you cannot reside for a year, unless you take first the monastic vow." When those who were present heard these words addressed to strangers who were only newly arrived they wondered very much. But the elder brother, in answer to the saint's remarks, replied, " Although we never up to the present hour entertained the thought before, yet we shall follow thy advice, believing that it cometh from God." What more need I say ? That very moment they entered the chapel with the saint, and on bended knees devoutly took the monastic vow. The saint then turned to his monks and said, " These two strangers who are presenting them-selves ' a living sacrifice to God,' and within a short time are fulfilling a long time of Christian warfare, shall pass away in peace this very month to Christ our Lord." The two brothers, on hearing this, gave thanks to God, and were led away to the guest-room. After seven days the elder brother fell sick, and departed to the Lord in the course of that week. After other seven days the other brother also fell sick, and within the same week passed to the Lord with joy, so that, according to the truthful prophecy of the saint, both closed their lives in this world within the space of one month.

CHAPTER XXVII.

The Prophecy of the holy man regarding a certain Artbranan.

WHEN the blessed man was staying for some days in the Scian island (Sky), he struck a spot of ground near the sea with his staff, and said to his companions : " Strange to say, my children, this day, an aged heathen, whose natural goodness has been preserved through all his life, will receive baptism, die, and be buried on this very spot." And lo ! about an hour after, a boat came into the harbour, on whose prow sat a decrepit old man, the chief of the Geona cohort. Two young men took him out of the boat and laid him at the feet of the blessed man. After being instructed in the word of God by the saint through an interpreter, the old man believed, and was baptized at once by him, and when the baptism was duly administered, he instantly died on the same spot, according to the saint's prediction, and was buried there by his companions, who raised a heap of stones over his grave. This cairn may be seen still on the sea-coast, and the river in which he was baptized is called to this day by the inhabitants, Dobur Artbranan.

CHAPTER XXVIII.

Of the Boat that was removed by the Saint's order.

ANOTHER time, as the saint was travelling beyond the Dorsal ridge of Britain (Drumalban), he came to a small village, lying amid deserted fields, on the banks of a river, where it flows into a lake. There the saint took up his abode, and that same night, while they were yet but falling asleep, he awoke his companions, and said to them : " Go out this instant with all speed, bring hither quickly the boat you left on the other side of the stream, and put it in a house near us." They did at once as they were ordered, and soon after they were again asleep, the saint roused Diormit, and said to him : "Stand outside the door, and see what has happened to the village in which you had left your boat." Diormit went out accordingly and saw the whole village on fire, and returning to the saint he told him what was taking place. Then the saint told the brethren the name of the rancorous foe who had burnt the houses that night.

CHAPTER XXIX.

*O Gallan, son of Fachtna, who resided in the jurisdiction of
Colga, son of Cellach.*

ONE day again, as the saint was sitting in his little hut, he
said, in prophecy to the same Colca, then reading by his side,
"Just now demons are dragging with them down to hell one of
the chiefs of thy district who is a niggardly person." When
Colca heard this, he marked the time accurately in a tablet,
and, coming home within a few months, learned on inquiry
from the inhabitants of the place, that Gallan, son of Fachtna,
died at the very moment that the saint said to him the man
was being carried off by demons.

*The Prophecy of the blessed man regarding Findchan, a Priest,
and the founder of the monastery called in Scotic Artchain,
in the Ethican land (Tiree).*

AT another time Findchan, the priest and soldier of Christ,
named above, brought with him from Scotia (Ireland) to Britain,
Aid, surnamed the Black, descended of a royal family, and a Cru-
thinian by race. Aid wore the clerical habit, and came with the
purpose of residing with him in the monastery for some years.
Now this Aid the Black had been a very bloodthirsty man, and
cruelly murdered many persons, amongst others Diormit, son of
Cerbul, by divine appointment king of all. This same Aid,
then, after spending some time in his retirement, was irregularly
ordained priest by a bishop invited for the purpose, in the presence of the above-named Findchan. The bishop, however,
would not venture to lay a hand upon his head unless Findchan,
who was greatly attached to Aid, in a carnal way, should first
place his right hand on his head as a mark of approval. When
such an ordination afterwards became known to the saint, he
was deeply grieved, and in consequence forthwith pronounced
this fearful sentence on the ill-fated Findchan and Aid: "That
right hand which, against the laws of God and the Church,
Findchan placed on the head of the son of perdition, shall soon
be covered with sores, and after great and excruciating pain
shall precede himself to the grave, and he shall survive the
burial of his hand for many years. And Aid, thus irregularly
ordained, shall return as a dog to his vomit, and be again a
bloody murderer, until at length, pierced in the neck with a
spear, he shall fall from a tree into the water and be drowned."

Such indeed was the end long due to him who murdered the king of all Scotia (Ireland). The blessed man's prophecy was fulfilled regarding both, for the priest Findchan's right hand festered from the effects of a blow, and went before him into the ground, being buried in an island called Ommon (not identified), while he himself survived for many years, according to the saying of St. Columba. But Aid the Black, a priest only in name, betaking himself again to his former evil doings, and being treacherously wounded with a spear, fell from the prow of a boat into a lake and was drowned.

Of the Consolation which the Monks, when they were weary on their journey, received from the Saint visiting them in spirit.

AMONG these wonderful manifestations of prophetical spirit it does not seem alien from the purpose of our short treatise to mention also here the spiritual comfort which the monks of St. Columba at one time received from his spirit's meeting them by the way. For as the brethren, on one occasion after the harvest work, were returning in the evening to the monastery, and came to a place called in Scotic Cuuleilne, which is said to lie on the western side of the Iouan island (Hy, now Iona), midway between the field on the plain and our monastery, each of them thought he felt something strange and unusual, which, however, they did not venture to speak of to one another. And so they had the same feeling for some days successively, at the same place, and at the same hour in the evening.

The holy Baithen at that particular time had charge of the work, and one day he said to them: "Now, my brethren, if any of you ever notices anything wonderful and unusual in this spot which lies between the corn-field and the monastery, it is your duty to declare it openly." An elder brother said, "As you have ordered me, I shall tell you what I observed on this spot. For both in the past few days, and even now, I perceive the fragrance of such a wonderful odour, just as if all the flowers on earth were gathered together into one place; I feel also a glow of heat within me, not at all painful, but most pleasing, and a certain unusual and inexpressible joy poured into my heart, which on a sudden so refreshes and gladdens me, that I forget grief and weariness of every kind. Even the load, however heavy, which I carry on my back, is in some mysterious way so much lightened, from this place all the way to the monastery, that I do not seem to have any weight to bear." What need I add? All the other reapers in turn declared they had exactly the same feeling as the first had described. All then knelt down together, and requested of the holy Baithen that he would learn and inform them of the as yet unknown cause and origin of this wonderful relief, which both he and they were feeling. " Ye all know," he immediately replied, "our father Columba's tender care regarding us, and how, ever mindful of our toil, he is always grieved when we return later than usual to the monastery. And now because he cannot come in person on this occasion to meet us, his spirit cometh forth to us as we walk along, and conveyeth to us such great comfort." Having heard these words, they raised their hands to heaven with intense joy as they knelt, and venerated Christ in the holy and blessed man.

I must not pass over another well-authenticated story, told, indeed, by those who heard it, regarding the voice of the blessed man in singing the psalms. The venerable man, when singing in the church with the brethren, raised his voice so wonderfully that it was sometimes heard four furlongs off, that is five hundred paces, and sometimes eight furlongs, that is one thousand paces. But what is stranger still : to those who were with him in the church, his voice did not seem louder than that of others ; and yet at the same time persons more than a mile away heard it so distinctly that they could mark each syllable of the verses he was singing, for his voice sounded the same whether far or near. It is however admitted, that this wonderful character in the voice of the blessed man was but rarely observable, and even then it could never happen without the aid of the Holy Ghost.

But another story concerning the great and wonderful power of his voice should not be omitted. The fact is said to have taken place near the fortress of King Brude (near Inverness). When the saint himself was chanting the evening hymns with a few of the brethren, as usual, outside the king's fortifications, some Druids, coming near to them, did all they could to prevent God's praises being sung in the midst of a pagan nation. On seeing this, the saint began to sing the 44th Psalm, and at the same moment so wonderfully loud, like pealing thunder, did his voice become, that king and people were struck with terror and amazement.

CHAPTER XXX.

Concerning a rich man named Lugud Clodus.

AT another time, when the saint was staying some days in Scotia (Ireland), he saw a cleric mounted on a chariot, and driving pleasantly along the plain of Breg (Magh Bregh, in Meath). On asking who the person was, the cleric's friend made this reply regarding him : " This is Lugud Clodus, who is rich, and much respected by the people." The saint immediately answered, " He does not seem so to me, but a poor wretched creature, who on the day of his death shall have within his own walled enclosure three of his neighbour's cattle which have strayed on to his property. The best of the strayed cows he shall order to be killed for his own use, and a part of the meat he shall direct to be cooked and served up to him at the very time that he is lying on the same couch with a prostitute, but by the first morsel that he eats shall he be choked and die immediately." Now all these things, as we heard from well-informed persons, afterwards happened according to the saint's prophecy.

CHAPTER XXXI.

Prophecy of the Saint regarding Neman, son of Gruthrich.

FOR when the saint corrected this man for his faults, he received the saint's reproof with derision. The blessed man then said to him, " In God's name I will declare these words of truth concerning thee, Neman, that thine enemies shall find thee in bed with a prostitute and put thee to death, and the evil spirits shall carry off thy soul to the place of torments." A few years after his enemies found this same Neman on a couch along with a prostitute, in the district of Cainle (not identified), and beheaded him, as was foretold by the saint.

CHAPTER XXXII.

Prophecy of the holy man regarding a certain Priest.

AT another time, as the saint was staying in that part of Scotia (Ireland), named a little before, he came by chance on the Lord's day to a neighbouring little monastery, called in the Scotic language Trioit (Trevet, in Meath). The same day a priest celebrated the holy mysteries of the Eucharist, who was selected by the brethren who lived there to perform the solemn offices of the Mass, because they thought him very pious. The saint, on hearing him, suddenly opened his mouth and uttered this fearful sentence : " The clean and unclean are now equally mingled together ; that is, the clean mysteries of the holy sacrifice are offered by an unclean person, who

just now conceals within his own conscience a grievous crime."
The bystanders, hearing these words, were struck with terror;
but he of whom they were said was forced to confess his sin
before them all. And the fellow-soldiers of Christ, who stood
round the saint in the church, and had heard him making mani-
fest the secrets of the heart, greatly wondered, and glorified the
heavenly knowledge that was seen in him.

CHAPTER XXXIII.

*The Prophecy of the holy man regarding the robber Erc Mocu-
druidi, who dwelt in the island Coloso (Colonsay).*

AT another time, when the saint was in the Iouan island (Hy,
now Iona), he called two of the brothers, Lugbe and Silnan, and
gave them this charge, " Sail over now to the Malean island
(Mull), and on the open ground, near the sea-shore, look for Erc,
a robber, who came alone last night in secret from the island
Coloso (Colonsay). He strives to hide himself among the sand-
hills during the daytime under his boat, which he covers with
hay, that he may sail across at night to the little island where
our young seals are brought forth and nurtured. When this
furious robber has stealthily killed as many as he can, he then
fills his boat, and goes back to his hiding-place." They proceeded at once in compliance with their orders, and found the
robber lying hid in the very spot that was indicated, and they
brought him to the saint, as they had been told. The saint
looked at him, and said, " Why dost thou transgress the com-
mandment of God so often by stealing the property of others ?
If thou art in want at any time, come to us and thy needs shall
be supplied." At the same time he ordered some wethers to
be killed, and given to the wretched thief in place of the seals,
that he might not return empty. A short time after the saint
saw in spirit that the death of the robber was at hand, and
ordered Baithen, then steward in the plain of Lunge (Maigh
Lunge, in Tiree), to send a fat sheep and six pecks of corn as a
last gift. Baithen sent them at once as the saint had recommended, but he found that the wretched robber had died suddenly the same day, and the presents sent over were used at
his burial.

CHAPTER XXXIV.

Prophecy of the holy man regarding the poet Cronan.

AT another time, as the saint was sitting one day with the
brothers beside the lake Ce (Lough Key, in Roscommon), at the

mouth of the river called in Latin Bos (the Boyle), a certain
Scotic poet came to them, and when he retired, after a short
interview, the brothers said to the saint, "Why didst thou not
ask the poet Cronan, before he went away, to sing us a song
with accompaniment, according to the rules of his profession?"
The saint replied, "Why do even you now utter such idle
words? How could I ask that poor man to sing a song of
joy, who has now been murdered, and thus hastily has ended
his days, at the hands of his enemies?" The saint had no
sooner said these words than immediately a man cried out
from beyond the river, "That poet who left you in safety a few
minutes ago has just now been met and put to death by his
enemies." Then all that were present wondered very much,
and looked at one another in amazement.

CHAPTER XXXV.

*The holy man's Prophecy regarding the two Noblemen who died
of wounds mutually inflicted.*

AGAIN, at another time, as the saint was living in the Iouan
island (Hy, now Iona), on a sudden, while he was reading, and
to the great surprise of all, he moaned very heavily. Lugbe
Mocublai, who was beside him, on seeing this, asked the cause of
such sudden grief. The saint, in very great affliction, answered
him, "Two men of royal blood in Scotia (Ireland) have perished
of wounds mutually inflicted near the monastery called Cellrois,
in the province of the Maugdorna (Magheross, in Monaghan);
and on the eighth day from the end of this week, one shall
give the shout on the other side of the Sound, who has come
from Hibernia, and will tell you all as it happened. But
oh! my dear child, tell this to nobody so long as I live." On
the eighth day, accordingly, the voice was heard beyond the
firth. Then the saint called quietly to Lugbe, and said to
him, "This is the aged traveller to whom I alluded, who
now crieth aloud beyond the strait; go and bring him here to
me." The stranger was speedily brought, and told, among
other things, how two noblemen in the district of the Maugdorna, near the confines of the territory in which is situate
the monastery of Cellrois, died of wounds received in single
combat—namely, Colman the Hound, son of Ailen, and Ronan,
son of Aid, son of Colga, both descended of the kings of
the Anteriores (the Airtheara, or people of Oriel in Ulster).
After these things were thus narrated, Lugbe, the soldier of
Christ, began to question the saint in private. "Tell me, I

entreat of thee, about these and such like prophetic revelations, how they are made to thee, whether by sight or hearing, or other means unknown to man." To this the saint replied, "Thy question regardeth a most difficult subject, on which I can give thee no information whatever, unless thou first strictly promise, on thy bended knees, by the name of the Most High God, never to communicate this most secret mystery to any person all the days of my life." Hearing this, Lugbe fell at once on his knees, and, with face bent down to the ground, promised everything faithfully as the saint demanded. After this pledge had been promptly given he arose, and the saint said to him, "There are some, though very few, who are enabled by divine grace to see most clearly and distinctly the whole compass of the world, and to embrace within their own wondrously enlarged mental capacity the utmost limits of the heavens and the earth at the same moment, as if all were illumined by a single ray of the sun." In speaking of this miracle, the saint, though he seems to be referring to the experience of other favoured persons, yet was in reality alluding to his own, though indirectly, that he might avoid the appearance of vain-glory; and no one can doubt this who reads the apostle Paul, that vessel of election, when he relates the visions revealed to himself. For he did not write, "I know that I," but "I know a man caught up even to the third heavens." Now, although the words seem strictly to refer to another person, yet all admit that he spoke thus of none but himself in his great humility. This was the model followed by our Columba in relating those visions of the Spirit spoken of above, and that, too, in such a way that even Lugbe, for whom the saint showed a special affection, could hardly force him to tell these wonders after much entreaty. And to this fact Lugbe himself, after St. Columba's death, bore witness in the presence of other holy men, from whom I learned the undoubted truths which I have now related of the saint.

Of Cronan the Bishop.

AT another time, a stranger from the province of the Munstermen, who in his humility did all he could to disguise himself, so that nobody might know he was a bishop, came to the saint; but his rank could not be hidden from the saint. For next Lord's day, being invited by the saint, as the custom was, to consecrate the Body of Christ, he asked the saint to join him, that, as two priests, they might break the bread of the Lord together. The saint went to the altar accordingly, and suddenly

looking into the stranger's face, thus addressed him : " Christ
bless thee, brother; do thou break the bread alone, according
to the episcopal rite, for I know now that thou art a bishop.
Why hast thou disguised thyself so long, and prevented our
giving thee the honour we owe to thee ? " On hearing the
saint's words, the humble stranger was greatly astonished, and
adored Christ in His saint, and the bystanders in amazement
gave glory to God.

The Saint's prophecy regarding Ernan the Priest.

AT another time, the venerable man sent Ernan, his uncle,
an aged priest, to preside over the monastery he had founded
many years before in Hinba island (Eilean-na-Naoimh). On
his departure the saint embraced him affectionately, blessed
him, and then foretold what would by and by happen to him,
saying, " This friend of mine, who is now going away from me, I
never expect to see alive again in this world." After a few days
this same Ernan became very unwell, and desired to be taken
back to the saint, who was much rejoiced at his return, and set
out for the harbour to meet him. Ernan also himself, though
with feeble step, attempted very boldly, and without assistance,
to walk from the harbour to meet him ; but when there was only
the short distance of twenty-four paces between them, death
came suddenly upon him before the saint could see his face in
life, and he breathed his last as he fell to the ground, that the
word of the saint might be fulfilled. Hence on that spot,
before the door of the kiln, a cross was raised, and another
cross was in like manner put up where the saint resided at the
time of his death, which remaineth unto this day.

The Saint's prophecy regarding the Family of a certain Peasant.

AT another time, when the saint was staying in that district
which is called in the Scotic tongue Coire Salchain (Corrie Sal-
lachan, now Corry, in Morvern), the peasants came to him, and
one evening when he saw one of them approaching he said to
him, " Where dost thou live ? " " I live," said he, " in that district which borders the shore of Lake Crogreth (Loch Creran).'
" That district of which thou speakest," replied the saint, " is
now being pillaged by savage marauders." On hearing this, the
unhappy peasant began to lament his wife and children; but
when the saint saw him so much afflicted he consoled him,
saying, " Go, my poor man, go ; thy whole family hath escaped
by flight to the mountains, but thy cattle, furniture, and other

effects the ruthless invaders have taken off with their unjust spoils." When the poor man heard these words he went home, and found that all had happened exactly as the saint foretold.

The Saint's prophecy regarding a Peasant called Goire, son of Aidan.

AT another time, in the same way, a peasant, who at that time was by far the bravest of all the inhabitants of Korkureti (Corkaree, in Westmeath), asked the saint by what death he would die. " Not in the battle-field shalt thou die," said the saint, " nor at sea; but the travelling companion of whom thou hast no suspicion shall cause thy death." " Perhaps," said Goire, " one of the friends who accompany me on my journey may be intending to murder me, or my wife, in her love for some younger man, may treacherously kill me." " Not so," replied the saint. " Why," asked Goire, " wilt thou not tell now the cause of my death?" " Because," said the saint, " I do not wish to tell more clearly just now the companion that is to injure thee, lest the frequent thought of the fact should make thee too unhappy, until the hour come when thou shalt find that my words are verified. Why dwell longer on what I have said?" After the lapse of a few years, this same Goire happened to be lying one day under his boat scraping off the bark from a spear-handle, when he heard others fighting near him. He rose hastily to stop the fighting, but his knife, through some neglect in the rapid movement, fell to the ground, and made a very deep wound in his knee. By such a companion, then, was his death caused, and he himself at once remembered with surprise the holy man's prophecy. After a few months he died, carried off by that same wound.

The Saint's foreknowledge and prophecy concerning a matter of less moment, but so beautiful that it cannot, I think, be passed over in silence.

FOR at another time, while the saint was living in the Iouan island (Hy, now Iona), he called one of the brothers, and thus addressed him : " In the morning of the third day from this date thou must sit down and wait on the shore on the western side of this island, for a crane, which is a stranger from the northern region of Hibernia, and hath been driven about by various winds, shall come, weary and fatigued, after the ninth hour, and lie down before thee on the beach quite exhausted. Treat that bird tenderly, take it to some neighbouring house, where it may be kindly received and carefully nursed and fed by thee for three days and three nights. When the crane is refreshed with the three days' rest, and is unwilling to abide any longer with us, it shall fly back with renewed strength to the pleasant part of Scotia (Ireland) from which it originally hath come. This bird do I consign to thee with such special care because it cometh from our own native place." The brother obeyed, and on the third day, after the ninth hour, he watched as he was bid for the arrival of the expected guest. As soon as the crane came and alighted on the shore, he took it up gently in its weakness, and carried it to a dwelling that was near, where in its hunger he fed it. On his return to the monastery in the evening, the saint, without any inquiry, but as stating a fact, said to him, " God bless thee, my child, for thy kind attention to this foreign visitor, that shall not remain long on its journey, but return within three days to its old home." As the saint predicted, so exactly did the event prove, for after being nursed carefully for three days, the bird then gently rose on its wings to a great height in the sight of its hospitable entertainer, and marking for a little its path through the air homewards, it directed its course across the sea to Hibernia, straight as it could fly, on a calm day.

The blessed man's foreknowledge regarding the Battle fought many years after in the fortress of Cethirn, and regarding the Well near that place.

ANOTHER time, after the convention of the kings at the Ridge of Ceate (Druim Ceatt)—that is, of Aidan, son of Gabran, and Aid, son of Ainmure—the blessed man returned to the sea-coast, and on a calm day in summer he and the Abbot Comgell sat down not far from the above-named fort. Then water was brought in a bronze vessel to the saints from a well that was close by to wash their hands. When St. Columba had received the water, he thus spoke to Abbot Comgell, who was sitting at his side, " A day shall come, O Comgell! when the well whence this water now poured out for us was drawn will be no longer fit for man's use." " How ?" said Comgell ; " shall the water of this spring be defiled ? " " From this," said St. Columba, " that it shall be filled with human blood ; for thy relatives and mine— that is, the people of the Cruithni and the race of Niall—shall be at war in the neighbouring fortress of Cethirn (now called the Giant's Sconce, near Coleraine). Whence, at this same well, an unhappy relative of mine shall be slain, and his blood, mingling with that of many others, shall fill it up." This truthful prophecy was duly accomplished after many years, for in that battle, as is well known to many, Domnall, son of Aid, came off victorious, and at that well, according to the saint's word, a near kinsman of his was slain.

Another soldier of Christ, called Finan, who led the life of an anchorite blamelessly for many years near the monastery of the Oakwood Plain (Derry), and who was present at the battle, in relating these things to me, Adamnan, assured me that he saw a man's dead body lying in the well, and that on his return from the battle-field the same day to the monastery of St. Comgell, which is called in the Scotic tongue Cambas (on the river Bann, in diocese of Derry), and from which he had first set out, he found there two aged monks, of St. Comgell, who, when he told them of the battle he saw, and of the well defiled with human blood, at once said to him: "A true prophet is Columba, for he foretold all the circumstances you now mention to-day regarding the battle and the well, many years indeed before they occurred; this he did in our hearing to St. Comgell, as he sat by the fort Cethirn."

How the Saint was favoured by God's grace with the power of distinguishing different Presents.

ABOUT the same time Conall, bishop of Culerathin (Coleraine), collected almost countless presents from the people of the plain of Eilne (Magh Elne, on the Bann), to give a hospitable reception to the blessed man, and the vast multitude that accompanied him, on his return from the meeting of the kings mentioned above.

Many of these presents from the people were laid out in the paved court of the monastery, that the holy man might bless them on his arrival; and as he was giving the blessing he specially pointed out one present, the gift of a wealthy man. "The mercy of God," said he, "attendeth the man who gave this, for his charity to the poor and his munificence." Then he pointed out another of the many gifts, and said: "Of this wise and avaricious man's offering, I cannot partake until he repent sincerely of his sin of avarice." Now this saying was quickly circulated among the crowd, and soon reaching the ears of Columb, son of Aid, his conscience reproached him; and he ran immediately to the saint, and on bended knees repented of his sin, promising to forsake his former greedy habits, and to be liberal ever after, with amendment of life. The saint bade him rise: and from that moment he was cured of the fault of greediness, for he was truly a wise man, as was revealed to the saint through that present.

But the munificent rich man, called Brenden, of whose present mention was made above, hearing the words of the saint regarding himself, knelt down at his feet and besought him to pray for him to the Lord. When at the outset the saint reproved him for certain other sins of which he was guilty, he expressed his heartfelt sorrow, and purpose of amendment. And thus both these men were cured of the peculiar vices in which they were wont to indulge. With like knowledge at another time, on the occasion of his visit to the Great Cell of Deathrib (Kilmore, in Roscommon), the saint knew the offering of a stingy man, called Diormit, from many others collected in that place on his arrival.

To have written thus much in the course of this first Book, selecting a few instances out of many of the prophetic gifts of the blessed man, may suffice. Indeed, I have recorded only a few facts regarding this venerable person, for no doubt there were very many more which could not come to men's knowledge, from being hidden under a kind of sacramental character, while those mentioned were like a few little drops which oozed out, as it were, like newly fermented wine through the chinks of a full vessel. For holy and apostolic men, in general, in order to avoid vain-glory, strive as much as they can to conceal the wonders of God's secret working within them. Yet God sometimes, whether they will or no, maketh some of these known to the world, and bringeth them into view by various means, wishing thus, as He doth, to honour those saints who honour Him, that is, our Lord Himself, to whom be glory for ever, and ever.

Here endeth this first Book, and the next Book treateth of the wonderful miracles, which generally accompanied his prophetic foreknowledge.

BOOK II.

ON HIS MIRACULOUS POWERS.

CHAPTER I.

Of the Wine which was formed from water.

AT another time, while the venerable man was yet a youth in Scotia (Ireland) learning the wisdom of the Holy Scripture under St. Findbarr, the bishop, it happened that on a festival day not the least drop of wine could be found for the mystic sacrifice. Hearing the ministers of the altar complaining among themselves of this want, he took the vessel and went to the fountain, that, as a deacon, he might bring pure spring water for the celebration of the Holy Eucharist; for at that time he was himself serving in the order of deacon. The holy man then blessed in faith that element of water taken from the spring, invoking, as he did so, the name of our Lord Jesus Christ, who in Cana of Galilee had changed water into wine: and the result was that by His operation in this miracle also, an inferior element, namely pure water, was changed into one of a more excellent kind, namely wine, by the hands of this illustrious man. The holy man, then returning from the fountain and entering the church, placed beside the altar the vessel containing this liquid, and said to the ministers: " Here is wine, which the Lord Jesus hath sent, for the celebration of His mysteries." The holy bishop and his ministers having ascertained the fact, returned most ardent thanks to God. But the holy youth ascribed this, not to himself, but to the holy bishop Vinnian. This first proof of miraculous power, Christ the Lord manifested in His disciple, just as under like circumstances He had made it the first of His own miracles in Cana of Galilee.

Let this divine miracle, worked by our Columba, shine as a light in the beginning of this book, that it may lead us on to the other divine and miraculous powers which were seen in him.

CHAPTER II.

Of the bitter fruit of a tree changed into sweet by the blessing of the Saint.

THERE was a certain very fruitful apple-tree on the south side of the monastery of the Oakwood Plain (Derry), in its immediate vicinity. When the inhabitants of the place were complaining of the exceeding bitterness of the fruit, the saint, one day in autumn, came to it, and seeing the boughs bearing to no purpose a load of fruit that injured rather than pleased those who tasted it, he raised his holy hand and blessed it, saying, "In the name of the Almighty God, O bitter tree, let all thy bitterness depart from thee; and let all thy apples, hitherto so very bitter, be now changed into the sweetest." Wonderful to be told, quicker than the word, and at that very instant, all the apples of the tree lost their bitterness, and were changed to an amazing sweetness, according to the saint's word.

CHAPTER III.

Of Corn sown after Midsummer and reaped in the beginning of the month of August, at the Saint's prayer, while he was residing in the Iouan island (Hy, now Iona).

AT another time the saint sent his monks to bring from the little farm of a peasant some bundles of twigs to build a dwelling. When they returned to the saint, with a freight-ship laden with the foresaid bundles of twigs, they told the saint that the poor man was very sorry on account of the loss. The saint immediately gave them these directions, saying, "Lest we do the man any wrong, take to him from us twice three measures of barley, and let him sow it now in his arable land." According to the saint's orders, the corn was sent and delivered over to the poor man, who was called Findchan, with the above directions. He received them with thanks, but asked, "What good can any corn do, which is sown after midsummer, against the nature of this soil?" But his wife, on the contrary, said, "Do what thou hast been ordered by the saint, to whom the Lord will give whatever he asketh from Him." And the messengers likewise said further, "St. Columba, who sent us to thee with this gift, intrusted us also with this form of instruction

regarding thy crop, saying, 'Let that man trust in the omnipotence of God; his corn, though sown now, when twelve
days of the month of June are passed, shall be reaped in the
beginning of the month of August.'" The peasant accordingly
ploughed and sowed, and the crop which, against hope, he sowed
at the above-mentioned time he gathered in ripe, to the admiration of all his neighbours, in the beginning of the month of
August, in that place which is called Delcros (not identified).

CHAPTER IV.

Of a Pestilential Cloud, and the curing of many.

AT another time also, while the saint was living in the Iouan
island (Hy, now Iona), and was sitting on the little hill which is
called, in Latin, Munitio Magna, he saw in the north a dense rainy
cloud rising from the sea on a clear day. As the saint saw it
rising, he said to one of his monks, named Silnan, son of Neman-
don Mocusogin, who was sitting beside him, "This cloud will
be very baleful to man and beast, and after rapidly passing to-
day over a considerable part of Scotia (Ireland)—namely, from
the stream called Ailbine (Delvin, in Meath) as far as the Ford
Clied (Athcliath, now Dublin)—it will discharge in the evening
a pestilential rain, which will raise large and putrid ulcers
on the bodies of men and on the udders of cows; so that men
and cattle shall sicken and die, worn out with that poisonous
complaint. But we, in pity for their sufferings, ought to relieve
them by the merciful aid of God; do thou therefore, Silnan,
come down with me from this hill, and prepare for thy to-
morrow's voyage. If God be willing and life spared to us, thou
shalt receive from me some bread which has been blessed by
the invocation of the name of God; this thou shalt dip in water,
and on thy sprinkling therewith man and beast, they shall
speedily recover their health." Why need we linger over it?
On the next day, when all things necessary had been hastily
got ready, Silnan received the blessed bread from the hands of
the saint, and set out on his voyage in peace. As he was
starting, the saint gave him these words of comfort, saying,
"Be of good courage, my dear son, for thou shalt have fair and
pleasant breezes day and night till thou come to that district
which is called Ard-Ceannachta (in Meath), that thou mayest
bring the more speedily relief with the healing bread to those
who are there sick." What more? Silnan, obeying the saint's
words, had a quick and prosperous voyage, by the aid of God,

and coming to the above-mentioned part of the district, found the
people of whom the saint had been speaking destroyed by the
pestilential rain falling down from the aforesaid cloud, which
had passed rapidly on before him.   In the first place, twice
three men were found in the same house near the sea reduced
to the agonies of approaching death, and when they were
sprinkled by Silnan with the blessed water, were very happily
healed that very day.   The report of this sudden cure was soon
carried through the whole country which was attacked by this
most fatal disease, and drew all the sick people to St. Columba's
messenger, who, according to the saint's orders, sprinkled man
and beast with the water in which the blessed bread had been
dipped, and immediately they were restored to perfect health ;
then the people finding themselves and their cattle healed,
praised with the utmost expression of thankfulness Christ in
St. Columba.   Now, in the incidents here related these two
things, I think, are clearly associated—namely, the gift of prophecy regarding the cloud and the miraculous power in healing
the sick.   And to the truth of all these things, in every particular, the above-named Silnan, the soldier of Christ and
messenger of St. Columba, bore testimony in the presence of
the Abbot Segine and the other fathers.

CHAPTER V.

*Of Maugina the holy virgin, daughter of Daimen, who had
lived in Clochur, of the sons of Daimen (Clogher).*

AT another time, while the saint was staying in the Iouan
island (Hy, now Iona), he one day at prime called to him a certain
brother, named Lugaid, who in the Scotic tongue was surnamed
Lathir, and thus addressed him, saying, " Prepare quickly for
a rapid voyage to Scotia (Ireland), for it is of the very utmost
importance to me that thou be sent with a message from me
to Clocher, of the sons of Daimen (Clogher).   For this last
night, by some accident, the holy virgin Maugina, daughter of
Daimen, when she was returning home from the oratory after
mass, stumbled and broke her thigh quite through.   She is now
crying out, and very often calling on my name, in hope that
through me she may receive some comfort from the Lord."
What more need I say ?   As Lugaid was setting out in
accordance with the directions given him, the saint gave him
a little box made of pine, saying, " Let the blessed gift
which is contained in this little box be dipped in a vessel

of water when thou comest to visit Maugina, and let the water thus blessed be poured on her thigh; then at once, by the invocation of God's name, her thigh-bone shall be joined together and made strong, and the holy virgin shall recover perfect health." This, too, the saint added, "Lo! here in thy presence I write on the lid of this little box the number of twenty-three years, which the holy virgin shall enjoy of this present life after receiving her health." All this was exactly fulfilled as the saint had foretold; for as soon as Lugaid came to the holy virgin her thigh was washed, as the saint recommended, with the blessed water, and was in an instant completely healed by the closing up of the bone. At the arrival of the messenger of St. Columba, she expressed her joy in the most earnest thanksgiving, and, after recovering her health, she lived, according to the prophecy of the saint, twenty-three years in the constant practice of good works.

CHAPTER VI.

Of the Cures of various Diseases which took place in the Ridge of Ceate (Druimceatt).

WE have been told by well-informed persons that this man of admirable life, by invoking the name of Christ, healed the disorders of various sick persons in the course of that short time which he spent at the Ridge of Ceate (Druimceatt), when attending there the meeting of the kings. For either by his merely stretching out his holy hand, or by the sprinkling of the sick with the water blessed by him, or by their touching even the hem of his cloak, or by their receiving his blessing on anything, as, for instance, on bread or salt, and dipping it in water, they who believed recovered perfect health.

CHAPTER VII.

Of a lump of Salt blessed by the Saint, which could not be consumed by the fire.

ON another occasion also, Colga, son of Cellach, asked and obtained from the saint a lump of salt which he had blessed, for the cure of his sister, who had nursed him, and was now suffering from a very severe attack of ophthalmia. This same

sister and nurse having received such a blessed gift from the
hand of her brother, hung it up on the wall over her bed ; and
after some days it happened by accident that a destructive fire
entirely consumed the village where this took place, and with
others the house of the aforesaid woman.   Yet, strange to say,
in order that the gift of the blessed man might not be destroyed,
the portion of the wall from which it was suspended still stood
uninjured after the rest of the house had been burned down ;
nor did the fire venture to touch even the two uprights from
which the lump of salt was suspended.

CHAPTER VIII.

*Of a volume of a book in the Saint's handwriting which could
not be destroyed by water.*

I CANNOT think of leaving unnoticed another miracle which
once took place by means of the opposite element.   For many
years after the holy man had departed to the Lord, a certain
youth fell from his horse into the river which in Scotic is called
Boend (the Boyne), and, being drowned, was for twenty days
under the water.   When he fell he had a number of books
packed up in a leathern satchel under his arm ; and so, when
he was found after the above-mentioned number of days, he
still had the satchel of books pressed between his arm and
side.   When the body was brought out to the dry ground, and
the satchel opened, it was found to contain, among the volumes
of other books, which were not only injured, but even rotten,
a volume written by the sacred fingers of St. Columba ; and
it was as dry and wholly uninjured as if it had been enclosed
in a desk.

Of another Miracle in similar circumstances.

AT another time a book of hymns for the office of every day in
the week, and in the handwriting of St. Columba, having slipt,
with the leathern satchel which contained it, from the shoulder
of a boy who fell from a bridge, was immersed in a certain
river in the province of the Lagenians (Leinster).   This very book
lay in the water from the Feast of the Nativity of our Lord till
the end of the Paschal season, and was afterwards found on the
bank of the river by some women who were walking there : it
was brought by them in the same satchel, which was not only

soaked, but even rotten, to a certain priest named Iogenan, a Pict by race, to whom it formerly belonged. On opening the satchel himself, Iogenan found his book uninjured, and as clean and dry as if it had been as long a time in his desk, and had never fallen into the water. And we have ascertained, as undoubted truth, from those who were well informed in the matter, that the like things happened in several places with regard to books written by the hands of St. Columba—namely, that the books could suffer no injury from being immersed in water. But the account we have given of the above-mentioned book of Iogenan we have received from certain truthful, excellent, and honourable men, who saw the book itself, perfectly white and beautiful, after a submersion of so many days, as we have stated.

These two miracles, though wrought in matters of small moment, and shown in opposite elements—namely, fire and water,—redound to the honour of the blessed man, and prove his great and singular merits before the Lord.

CHAPTER IX.

Of Water drawn from the hard rock by the Saint's prayers.

AND since mention has been made a little before of the element of water, we must not pass over in silence some other miracles which the Lord wrought by the saint at different times and places, in which the same element was concerned. On another occasion, then, when the saint was engaged in one of his journeys, a child was presented to him in the course of his travels for baptism by its parents; and because there was no water to be found in the neighbourhood, the saint turned aside to a rock that was near, and kneeling down prayed for a short time; then rising up after his prayer, he blessed the face of the rock, from which there immediately gushed out an abundant stream of water; and there he forthwith baptized the child. Concerning the child that was baptized he uttered the following prophecy, saying, " This child shall live to a very great age; in his youth he will indulge freely the desires of the flesh; afterwards he will devote himself to the warfare of a Christian until the very end of his life, and thus depart to the Lord in a good old age." All this happened to the man according to the prophecy of the saint. This was Lugucencalad, whose parents were from Artdaib Muirchol (Ardnamurchan), where there is seen even to this day a well called by the name of St. Columba.

CHAPTER X.

Of a poisonous Fountain of Water to which the blessed man gave his blessing in the country of the Picts.

AGAIN, while the blessed man was stopping for some days in the province of the Picts, he heard that there was a fountain famous amongst this heathen people, which foolish men, having their senses blinded by the devil, worshipped as a god. For those who drank of this fountain, or purposely washed their hands or feet in it, were allowed by God to be struck by demoniacal art, and went home either leprous or purblind, or at least suffering from weakness or other kinds of infirmity. By all these things the Pagans were seduced, and paid divine honour to the fountain. Having ascertained this, the saint one day went up to the fountain fearlessly ; and, on seeing this, the Druids, whom he had often sent away from him vanquished and confounded, were greatly rejoiced, thinking that he would suffer like others from the touch of that baneful water. But he, having first raised his holy hand and invoked the name of Christ, washed his hands and feet; and then with his companions, drank of the water which he had blessed. And from that day the demons departed from the fountain ; and not only was it not allowed to injure any one, but even many diseases amongst the people were cured by this same fountain, after it had been blessed and washed in by the saint.

CHAPTER XI.

Of the Danger to the blessed man at Sea, and the sudden calm produced by his prayers.

AT another time the holy man began to be in great danger at sea, for the whole vessel was violently tossed and shaken with the huge dashing waves, and a great storm of wind was raging on all hands. The sailors then chanced to say to the saint, as he was trying to help them to bale the vessel, "What thou art now doing is of little use to us in our present danger, thou shouldst rather pray for us as we are perishing." On hearing this he ceased to throw out the bitter waters of the green sea wave, and began to pour out a sweet and fervent prayer to the Lord. Wonderful to relate ! The very moment the saint stood up at the prow, with his hands stretched out to heaven, and prayed to the Almighty, the whole storm of wind and the fury of the sea ceased more quickly than can be told, and a perfect calm instantly ensued. But those who were in the vessel were amazed, and giving thanks with great admiration, glorified the Lord in the holy and illustrious man.

CHAPTER XII.

Of another similar Peril to him at Sea.

AT another time, also, when a wild and dangerous storm was raging, and his companions were crying out to the saint to pray to the Lord for them, he gave them this answer, saying, " On this day it is not for me, but for that holy man, the Abbot Cainnech, to pray for you in your present peril." What I am to relate is wonderful. The very same hour St. Cainnech was in his monastery, which in Latin is called Campulus Bovis, but in Scotic Ached-bou (Aghaboe, in Queen's County), and heard with the inner ear of his heart, by a revelation of the Holy Ghost, the aforesaid words of St. Columba; and when he had just begun to break the blessed bread in the refectory after the ninth hour, he hastily left the table, and with one shoe on his foot, while the other in his extreme haste was left behind, he went quickly to the church, saying, " It is not for us now to take time to dine, when the vessel of St. Columba is in danger at sea, for at this moment he is lamenting and calling on the name of Cainnech to pray to Christ for him and his companions in peril." When he had said this he entered the oratory and prayed for a short time on his bended knees; and the Lord heard his prayer, the storm immediately ceased, and the sea became very calm. Whereupon St. Columba, seeing in spirit, though there was a far distance between them, the haste of Cainnech in going to the church, uttered, to the wonder of all, from his pure heart, these words, saying, " Now I know, O Cainnech, that God has heard thy prayer; now hath thy swift running to the church with a single shoe greatly profited us." In such a miracle as this, then, we believe that the prayers of both saints had their share in the work.

CHAPTER XIII.

Of the Staff of St. Cainnech which was forgotten in the Harbour.

ON another occasion, the same Cainnech above mentioned embarked for Scotia (Ireland) from the harbour of the Iouan island (Hy, now Iona), and forgot to take his staff with him. After

his departure the staff was found on the shore, and given into
the hands of St. Columba, who, on his return home, brought it
into the oratory, and remained there for a very long time alone
in prayer.   Cainnech, meanwhile, on approaching the Oidechan
island (Oidech, near Isla, probably Texa) suddenly felt pricked
at heart at the thought of his forgetfulness, and was deeply
afflicted at it.   But after some time, leaving the vessel, and
falling upon his knees in prayer on the ground, he found before
him on the turf of the little land of Aithche (genitive of Aitech)
the staff which, in his forgetfulness, he had left behind him at
the landing-place in the Iouan island (Hy, now Iona).   He was
greatly surprised at its being thus brought to him by the divine
power, and gave thanks to God.

CHAPTER XIV.

*How Baithene and Columban, the son of Beogna, holy priests,
asked of the Lord, through the prayers of the blessed man,
that he would grant them on the same day a favourable wind,
though sailing in different directions.*

AT another time, also, the above-named holy men came in
company to the saint, and asked him, with one consent, to seek
and obtain for them from the Lord a favourable wind on the
next day, though they were to set out in different directions.
The saint in answer gave them this reply, "To-morrow morning,
Baithene, setting sail from the harbour of the Iouan island (Hy,
now Iona), shall have a favourable wind until he reaches the
landing-place of the plain of Lunge (Magh Lunge, in Tiree)."
And the Lord granted this favour according to the word of the
saint; for Baithene on that same day crossed, with full sails,
the whole of the open sea, as far as the Ethican land (Tiree).
But at the third hour of the same day, the venerable man called
to him the priest Columban, saying, " Baithene has now
happily arrived at the wished-for haven, prepare thou then
to sail to-day; the Lord will soon change the wind to the
north."   And the same hour the wind from the south obeying the word thus spoken by the holy man, wheeled round
and became a northern breeze ; and thus on the same day
these two holy men departed the one from the other in peace
and both set sail, Baithene in the morning for the Ethican land
(Tiree), and Columban in the afternoon for Hibernia, and made
the voyages with full sails and fair winds.   The Lord wrought
this miracle in answer to the prayer of the illustrious man,
according as it is written, "All things are possible to him

that believeth." After the departure of St. Columban on that day, St. Columba uttered this prophecy concerning him : "The holy man, Columban, whom we have blessed on his departure, shall never see my face again in this world." And this was afterwards fulfilled, for the same year St. Columban passed away to the Lord.

CHAPTER XV.

Of the driving out of a Demon that lurked in a Milk-pail.

AT another time, a certain youth, named Columban, grandson of Brian, came forward hurriedly, and stopped at the door of the little cell in which the blessed man was writing. This same person, being on his way home from the milking of the cows, and carrying on his back a vessel full of new milk, asked the saint to bless his burden, as he usually did. Then the saint, being at the time at some distance away in front of him, raised his hand, and formed the saving sign in the air, which at once was greatly agitated ; the bar, which fastened the lid of the pail, being pushed back through the two openings that received it, was shot away to a great distance, while the lid fell to the earth, and the greater part of the milk was spilled upon the ground. The young lad then laid down the vessel, with the little milk that remained, on its bottom on the ground, and kneeled down in prayer. The saint said to him, " Rise up, Columban, for thou hast acted negligently in thy work to-day, inasmuch as thou didst not banish the demon that lurked in the bottom of the empty vessel by forming on it the sign of the cross of our Lord before the milk was poured into it ; and now, as thou seest, being unable to bear the power of that sign, he has quickly fled in terror, troubled the whole vessel in every corner, and spilled the milk. Bring the vessel, then, nearer to me here that I may bless it." This being done, the half-empty pail, which the saint had blessed, was found the same instant, filled by divine agency ; and the little that had previously remained in the bottom was at once increased under the blessing of his holy hand, so as to fill it to the brim.

CHAPTER XVI.

Concerning a Vessel which a sorcerer named Silnan had filled with milk taken from a bull.

THE following is told as having occurred in the house of a rich peasant named Foirtgirn, who lived in Mount Cainle (not identified).   When the saint was staying there, he decided justly a dispute between two rustics, whose coming to him he knew beforehand : and one of them, who was a sorcerer, took milk, by his diabolical art, at the command of the saint, from a bull that was near.   This the saint directed to be done, not to confirm these sorceries—God forbid ! but to put an end to them in the presence of all the people.   The blessed man, therefore, demanded that the vessel, full, as it seemed to be, of this milk, should be immediately given to him ; and he blessed it with this sentence, saying : " Now it shall in this way be proved that this is not true milk, as it is supposed to be, but blood, which is coloured by the artifice of demons to impose on men." This was no sooner said than the milky colour gave place to the true natural colour of blood.   The bull also, which in the space of one hour wasted and pined away with a hideous lean-ness, and was all but dead, was sprinkled with water that had been blessed by the saint, and recovered with astonishing rapidity.

CHAPTER XVII.

Of Lugne Mocumin.

ONE day a young man of good disposition and parts, named Lugne, who afterwards, in his old age, was prior of the monastery of the Elena island (Eilean Naomh, now Nave island, near Isla), came to the saint, and complained of a bleeding which for many months had often poured profusely from the nostrils.   Having asked him to come nearer, the saint pressed both his nostrils with two fingers of his right hand and blessed him.   And from that hour when he received the bless-ing, till the last day of his life, a drop of blood never came from his nose.

CHAPTER XVIII.

Of the Fishes which were specially provided by God for the blessed man.

ON another occasion, when some hardy fishermen, com-panions of this renowned man, had taken five fish in their net in the river Sale (the Shiel, or Seil), which abounds in fish, the saint said to them, " Try again," said he ; " cast thy net into the stream, and you shall at once find a large fish which the Lord has provided for me."   In obedience to the saint's command they hauled in their nets a salmon of astonishing size, which God had provided for him.

CHAPTER XIX.

AT another time also, when the saint was stopping some days beside the lake of Ce (Loughkey, in Roscommon), he delayed his companions when they were anxious to go a-fishing, saying: "No fish will be found in the river to-day or to-morrow; but on the third day I will send you, and you shall find two large river-salmon taken in the net." And so, after two short days, they cast their nets, and landed two, of the most extraordinary size, which they found in the river which is named Bo (the Boyle). In the capture of fish on these two occasions, the power of miracles appears accompanied at the same time by a prophetic foreknowledge, and for both graces the saint and his companions gave fervent thanks to God.

CHAPTER XX.

Regarding Nesan the Crooked, who lived in the country bordering on the Lake of Apors (Lochaber).

THIS Nesan, though very poor, joyfully received on one occasion the saint as his guest. And after he had entertained him as hospitably as his means would afford for one night, the saint asked him the number of his heifers. He answered, " Five." The saint then said, " Bring them to me that I may bless them." And when they were brought the saint raised his holy hand and blessed them, and said : " From this day thy five little heifers shall increase to the number of one hundred and five cows." And as this same Nesan was a man of humble condition, having a wife and children, the saint added this further blessing, saying: "Thy seed shall be blessed in thy children and grandchildren." And all this was completely fulfilled without any failure, according to the word of the saint.

CHAPTER XXI.

ON the other hand, he pronounced the following prophetic sentence on a certain rich and very stingy man named Uigene, who despised St. Columba, and showed him no hospitality, saying : " But the riches of that niggardly man who hath despised Christ in the strangers that came to be his guests, will gradually become less from this day, and be reduced to nothing; and he himself shall be a beggar ; and his son shall go about from house to house with a half-empty wallet : and he shall be slain by a rival beggar with an axe, in the pit of a threshing-floor." All this was exactly fulfilled in both cases, according to the prophecy of the holy man.

CHAPTER XXII.

How the holy man blessed the few Cattle belonging to Columban,
a man of equally humble condition; and how, after his
blessing, they increased to the number of a hundred.

AT another time also, the blessed man was one night kindly
treated as his guest by the aforesaid Columban, who was then
very poor, and, as he had done before in the above account of
Nesan, he asked his host, early next morning, as to the amount
and kind of his goods. When asked, he said: " I have only
five small cows, but if thou bless them they will increase to
more." And immediately he was directed by the saint to bring
them before him, and in the same manner as was related concerning the five cows of Nesan, he gave as rich a blessing to those of
Columban, and said, "Thou shalt have, by God's gift, a hundred
and five cows, and an abundant blessing shall be also upon thy
children and grandchildren." All this was granted to the full
in his lands, and cattle, and offspring, according to the prophecy
of the blessed man ; and, what is very strange, the number of
cattle determined by the saint for both these men, whenever it
reached one hundred and five, could not in any way be increased; for those that were beyond this stated number, being
carried off by various accidents, never appeared to be of any
value, except in so far as anything might be employed for the
use of the family, or spent in almsgiving. In this history,
then, as in the others, the gifts both of miracles and prophecy
are clearly shown together, for in the large increase of the
cattle we see the virtue of his blessing and of his prayer, and,
in the determination of the number, his prophetic knowledge.

CHAPTER XXIII.

Of the Death of some wicked men who had spurned the Saint.

THE venerable man had a great love for the above-named
Columban, on account of the many acts of kindness he had
done to him, and caused him by blessing him, from being poor
to become very rich. Now, there was at that time a certain
wicked man, a persecutor of the good, named Joan, son of
Conall, son of Domnall, sprung from the royal tribe of Gabran.
This man troubled the foresaid Columban, the friend of St.
Columba ; and not once, but twice, attacked and plundered his

house and carried off all he could find in it. Hence it not un-
fitly happened to this wicked man, that as he and his associates,
after having plundered the house of the same person a third
time, were returning to their vessel, laden with plunder, he met
advancing towards him, the holy man whom he had despised,
when he thought he was afar off. When the saint reproached
him for his evil deeds, and advised and besought him to give
up the plunder, he remained hardened and obstinate, and
scorned the holy man ; and thus mocking and laughing at the
blessed man, he embarked with the booty. Yet the saint
followed him to the water's edge, and wading up to the knees in
the clear green sea-water, with both his hands raised to heaven,
earnestly invoked Christ, who glorifies His elect, who are giving
glory to Him.

Now the haven where he thus for some time stood and besought the Lord after the departure of the oppressor, is at a
place called in Scotic Ait-Chambas Art-Muirchol (Camus-an-
Gaall, Ardnamurchan). Then the saint, as soon as he had finished
his prayer, returned to the dry ground, and sat down on the
higher ground with his companions, and spoke to them in
that hour these very terrible words, saying : "This miserable
wretch who' hath despised Christ in His servants will never
return to the port from which you have now seen him set sail :
neither shall he, nor his wicked associates, reach the land for
which they are bound, for a sudden death shall prevent it. This
day a furious storm shall proceed from a cloud, which you will
soon see rising in' the north, shall overwhelm him and his
companions, so that not one of them will survive to tell the
tale." After the lapse of a few moments, even while the day
was perfectly calm, behold ! a cloud arose from the sea, as the
saint had said, and caused a great hurricane, which overtook the
plunderer with his spoil, between the Malean and Colosus islands
(Mull and Colonsay), and overwhelmed him in the midst of the
sea, which was suddenly lashed into fury : and not even one of
those in the vessel escaped, as the saint had said : and in this
wonderful manner, by such a singular storm, while the whole
sea around remained quiet, were the robbers miserably, but
justly, overwhelmed and sunk into the deep.

CHAPTER XXIV.

Of a certain Feradach, who was cut off by sudden death.

AT another time also, the holy man specially recommended
a certain exile, of noble race among the Picts, named Tarain, to

the care of one Feradach, a rich man, who lived in the Ilean island
(Isla), that he might be received in his retinue for some months
as one of his friends. After he had accepted the person thus
highly recommended at the hand of the holy man, he in a few
days acted treacherously, and cruelly ordered him to be put to
death. When the news of this horrid crime was carried by
travellers to the saint, he replied by the following prediction:
" That unhappy wretch hath not lied unto me, but unto God,
and his name shall be blotted out of the book of life. We are
speaking these words now in the middle of summer, but in
autumn, before he shall eat of swine's flesh that hath been
fattened on the fruits of the trees, he shall be seized by a sudden
death, and carried off to the infernal regions." When the
miserable man was told this prophecy of the saint, he scorned
and laughed at him; and when some days of the autumn months
had passed, he ordered a sow that had been fattened on the
kernels of nuts to be killed, none of his other swine having yet
been slaughtered: he ordered also, that its entrails should be
immediately taken out and a piece quickly roasted for him on
the spit, so that by hurrying and eating of it thus early, he
might falsify the prediction of the blessed man. As soon as it
was roasted he asked for a very small morsel to taste it, but
before the hand which he stretched out to take it had reached
his mouth he expired, and fell down on his back a corpse. And
all who saw or heard it were greatly astonished and terrified;
and they honoured and glorified Christ in his holy prophet.

CHAPTER XXV.

*Concerning a certain other impious man, a persecutor of the
Churches, who was called in Latin Manus Dextera.*

On one occasion when the blessed man was living in the Hinba
island (Eilean-na-Naoimh), and set about excommunicating
some destroyers of the churches, and amongst them the sons of
Conall, son of Domnall, one of whom was the Joan before
mentioned, one of their wicked associates was instigated by
the devil to rush on the saint with a spear, on purpose to kill
him. To prevent this, one of the brethren, named Findlugan,
put on the saint's cowl and interposed, being ready to die
for the holy man. But in a wonderful way the saint's garment served as a kind of strong and impenetrable fence
which could not be pierced by the thrust of a very sharp

spear though made by a powerful man, but remained un-
touched, and he who had it on was safe and uninjured under
the protection of such a guard. But the ruffian who did this,
whose name was Manus Dextera, retraced his steps thinking he
had transfixed the saint with his spear. Exactly a year afterwards, when the saint was staying in the Iouan island (Hy,
now Iona), he said, " A year is just now elapsed since the day
Lam-dess did what he could to put Findlugan to death in my
place ; but he himself is slain, I believe, this very hour." And
so it happened, at that very moment, according to the revelation of the saint, in the island which in Latin may be called
Longa (Luing), where, in a battle fought between a number of
men on both sides, this Lam-dess alone was slain by Cronan,
son of Baithene, with a dart, shot, it is said, in the name of
St. Columba ; and when he fell the battle ceased.

CHAPTER XXVI.

Of yet another Oppressor of the innocent.

WHEN the holy man, while yet a youth in deacon's orders,
was living in the region of the Lagenians (Leinster), learning
the divine wisdom, it happened one day that an unfeeling and
pitiless oppressor of the innocent was pursuing a young girl who
fled before him on a level plain. As she chanced to observe the
aged Gemman, master of the foresaid young deacon, reading
on the plain, she ran straight to him as fast as she could.
Being alarmed at such an unexpected occurrence, he called
on Columba, who was reading at some distance, that both together, to the best of their ability, might defend the girl from
her pursuer ; but he immediately came up, and without any
regard to their presence, stabbed the girl with his lance under
their very cloaks, and leaving her lying dead at their feet
turned to go away back. Then the old man, in great affliction,
turning to Columba, said : " How long, holy youth Columba,
shall God, the just Judge, allow this horrid crime and this
insult to us to go unpunished ?" Then the saint at once
pronounced this sentence on the perpetrator of the deed :
" At the very instant the soul of this girl whom he hath murdered ascendeth into heaven, shall the soul of the murderer go
down into hell." And scarcely had he spoken the words when
the murderer of the innocent, like Ananias before Peter, fell
down dead on the spot before the eyes of the holy youth. The
news of this sudden and terrible vengeance was soon spread

abroad throughout many districts of Scotia (Ireland), and with it the wonderful fame of the holy deacon.

What we have said may suffice concerning the terrible punishments inflicted on those who were opposed to him; we will now relate a few things regarding wild beasts.

CHAPTER XXVII.

How a Wild Boar was destroyed through his prayers.

ON one occasion when the blessed man was staying some days in the Scian island (Sky), he left the brethren and went alone a little farther than usual to pray; and having entered a dense forest he met a huge wild boar that happened to be pursued by hounds. As soon as the saint saw him at some distance, he stood looking intently at him. Then raising his holy hand and invoking the name of God in fervent prayer, he said to it, " Thou shalt proceed no further in this direction: perish in the spot which thou hast now reached." At the sound of these words of the saint in the woods, the terrible brute was not only unable to proceed farther, but by the efficacy of his word immediately fell dead before his face.

CHAPTER XXVIII.

How an Aquatic Monster was driven off by virtue of the blessed man's prayer.

ON another occasion also, when the blessed man was living for some days in the province of the Picts, he was obliged to cross the river Nesa (the Ness); and when he reached the bank of the river, he saw some of the inhabitants burying an unfortunate man, who, according to the account of those who were burying him, was a short time before seized, as he was swimming, and bitten most severely by a monster that lived in the water; his wretched body was, though too late, taken out with a hook, by those who came to his assistance in a boat. The blessed man, on hearing this, was so far from being dismayed, that he directed one of his companions to swim over and row across the coble that was moored at the farther bank. And Lugne Mocumin hearing the command of the excellent man, obeyed without the.

least delay, taking off all his clothes, except his tunic, and leaping into the water.   But the monster, which, so far from being satiated, was only roused for more prey, was lying at the bottom of the stream, and when it felt the water disturbed above by the man swimming, suddenly rushed out, and, giving an awful roar, darted after him, with its mouth wide open, as the man swam in the middle of the stream.   Then the blessed man observing this, raised his holy hand, while all the rest, brethren as well as strangers, were stupefied with terror, and, invoking the name of God, formed the saving sign of the cross in the air, and commanded the ferocious monster, saying, " Thou shalt go no further, nor touch the man ; go back with all speed."   Then at the voice of the saint, the monster was terrified, and fled more quickly than if it had been pulled back with ropes, though it had just got so near to Lugne, as he swam, that there was not more than the length of a spear-staff between the man and the beast.   Then the brethren seeing that the monster had gone back, and that their comrade Lugne returned to them in the boat safe and sound, were struck with admiration, and gave glory to God in the blessed man.   And even the barbarous heathens, who were present, were forced by the greatness of this miracle, which they themselves had seen, to magnify the God of the Christians.

CHAPTER XXIX.

How the Saint blessed the Soil of this Island that no poison of Serpents should henceforth hurt any one in it.

ON a certain day in that same summer in which he passed to the Lord, the saint went in a chariot to visit some of the brethren, who were engaged in some heavy work in the western part of the Iouan island (Hy, now Iona).   After speaking to them some words of comfort and encouragement, the saint stood upon the higher ground, and uttered the following prophecy :— " My dear children, I know that from this day you shall never see my face again anywhere in this field."   Seeing the brethren filled with sorrow upon hearing these words, the saint tried to comfort them as best he could ; and, raising both his holy hands, he blessed the whole of this our island, saying :—" From this very moment poisonous reptiles shall in no way be able to hurt men or cattle in this island, so long as the inhabitants shall continue to observe the commandments of Christ."

CHAPTER XXX.

Of the Knife which the Saint blessed by signing it with the Lord's Cross.

At another time, a certain brother named Molua, grandson of Brian, came to the saint whilst he was writing, and said to him, "This knife which I hold in my hand I beseech thee to bless." The saint, without turning his face from the book out of which he was writing, extended his holy hand a little, with the pen in it, and blessed the knife by signing it. But when the foresaid brother had departed with the knife thus blessed, the saint asked, "What sort of a knife have I blessed for that brother?" Diormit, the saint's faithful attendant, replied, "Thou hast blessed a knife for killing bulls or oxen." The saint then, on the contrary, said, "I trust in my Lord that the knife I have blessed will never wound men or cattle." This word of the holy man received the strongest confirmation the same hour; for the same brother went beyond the enclosure of the monastery and attempted to kill an ox, but, although he made three strong efforts with all his strength, yet he could not even cut the skin. When this came to the knowledge of the monks, they skilfully melted down the iron of the knife and applied a thin coating of it to all the iron tools used in the monastery. And such was the abiding virtue of the saint's blessing, that these tools could never afterwards inflict a wound on flesh.

CHAPTER XXXI.

Of the cure of Diormit when sick.

At another time, Diormit, the saint's faithful attendant, was sick even unto death, and the saint went to see him in his extremity. Having invoked the name of Christ, he stood at the bed of the sick man and prayed for him, saying, "O my Lord, be propitious to me, I beseech thee, and take not away the soul of my faithful attendant from its dwelling in the flesh whilst I live." Having said this, he remained silent for a short time, and then again he spoke these words, with his sacred mouth, "My son shall not only not die at present, but will even live for many years after my death." This prayer of the saint was heard, for, on the instant that the saint's prayer was made, Diormit was restored to perfect health, and lived also for many years after St. Columba had passed to the Lord.

CHAPTER XXXII.

*Of the cure of Finten, the son of Aid, when at the point
of death.*

AT another time also, as the saint was making a journey
beyond the Dorsal Ridge of Britain (Drumalban), a certain
youth named Finten, one of his companions, was seized with a
sudden illness and reduced to the last extremity.   His comrades
were much afflicted on his account, and besought the saint to
pray for him.   Yielding at once to their entreaties, Columba
raised his holy hands to heaven in earnest prayer, and blessing
the sick person, said, " This youth for whom you plead shall
enjoy a long life ; he will survive all who are here present,
and die in a good old age."   This prophecy of the blessed man
was fulfilled in every particular ; for this same youth, after
founding the monastery of Kailli-au-inde (not identified), closed
this present life at a good old age.

CHAPTER XXXIII.

*Of the boy whom the holy man raised from the dead, in the
name of the Lord Christ.*

AT the time when St. Columba was tarrying for some days
in the province of the Picts, a certain peasant who, with his
whole family, had listened to and learned through an interpreter the word of life preached by the holy man, believed and
was baptized—the husband, together with his wife, children,
and domestics.

A very few days after his conversion, one of the sons of this
householder was attacked with a dangerous illness and brought
to the very borders of life and death.   When the Druids saw
him in a dying state they began with great bitterness to up-
braid his parents, and to extol their own gods as more powerful than the God of the Christians, and thus to despise God as
though He were weaker than their gods.   When all this was
told to the blessed man, he burned with zeal for God, and proceeded with some of his companions to the house of the friendly
peasant, where he found the afflicted parents celebrating the
obsequies of their child, who was newly dead.   The saint, on
seeing their bitter grief, strove to console them with words of
comfort, and exhorted them not to doubt in any way the omnipotence of God.   He then inquired, saying, " In what chamber

is the dead body of your son lying?" And being conducted by the bereaved father under the sad roof, he left the whole crowd of persons who accompanied him outside, and immediately entered by himself into the house of mourning, where, falling on his knees, he prayed to Christ our Lord, having his face bedewed with copious tears. Then rising from his kneeling posture, he turned his eyes towards the deceased and said, " In the name of the Lord Jesus Christ, arise, and stand upon thy feet." At the sound of this glorious word from the saint, the soul returned to the body, and the person that was dead opened his eyes and revived. The apostolic man then taking him by the hand raised him up, and placing him in a standing position, led him forth with him from the house, and restored him to his parents. Upon this the cries of the applauding multitude broke forth, sorrow was turned into joy, and the God of the Christians glorified.

We must thus believe that our saint had the gift of miracles like the prophets Elias and Eliseus, and like the apostles Peter, Paul, and John, he had the honour bestowed on him of raising the dead to life, and now in heaven, placed amid the prophets and apostles, this prophetic and apostolic man enjoys a glorious and eternal throne in the heavenly fatherland with Christ, who reigns with the Father in the unity of the Holy Ghost for ever and ever.

CHAPTER XXXIV.

Concerning the illness with which the Druid Broichan was visited for his detention of a female slave, and his cure on her release.

ABOUT the same time the venerable man, from motives of humanity, besought Broichan the Druid to liberate a certain Scotic female slave, and when he very cruelly and obstinately refused to part with her, the saint then spoke to him to the following effect :—" Know, O Broichan, and be assured that if thou refuse to set this captive free, as I desire thee, that thou shalt die suddenly before I take my departure again from this province." Having said this in presence of Brude, the king, he departed from the royal palace and proceeded to the river Nesa (the Ness); from this stream he took a white pebble, and showing it to his companions said to them :—" Behold this white pebble by which God will effect the cure of many diseases among this heathen nation."

Having thus spoken, he instantly added, " Broichan is chastised grievously at this moment, for an angel being sent from heaven, and striking him severely, hath broken into many pieces the glass cup in his hand from which he was drinking, and hath left him gasping deeply for breath, and half dead. Let us await here a short time, for two of the king's messengers, who have been sent after us in haste, to request us to return quickly and help the dying Broichan, who, now that he is thus terribly punished, consenteth to set the girl free."

Whilst the saint was yet speaking, behold, there arrived, as he had predicted, two horsemen who were sent by the king, and who related all that had occurred to Broichan in the royal fortress, according to the prediction of the saint—both the breaking of the drinking goblet, the punishment of the Druid, and his willingness to set his captive at liberty; they then added: "The king and his friends have sent us to thee to request that thou wouldst cure his foster-father Broichan, who lieth in a dying state.

Having heard these words of the messengers, St. Columba sent two of his companions to the king with the pebble which he had blessed, and said to them :—" If Broichan shall first promise to set the maiden free, then at once immerse this little stone in water, and let him drink from it and he shall be instantly cured; but if he break his vow and refuse to liberate her, he shall die that instant."

The two persons, in obedience to the saint's instructions, proceeded to the palace, and announced to the king the words of the venerable man. When they were made known to the king and his tutor Broichan, they were so dismayed that they immediately liberated the captive and delivered her to the saint's messengers. The pebble was then immersed in water, and in a wonderful manner, contrary to the laws of nature, the stone floated on the water like a nut or an apple, nor, as it had been blessed by the holy man, could it be submerged. Broichan drank from the stone as it floated on the water, and instantly returning from the verge of death recovered his perfect health and soundness of body.

This remarkable pebble, which was afterwards preserved among the treasures of the king, through the mercy of God effected the cure of sundry diseases among the people, while it in the same manner floated when dipped in water. And what is very wonderful, when this same stone was sought for by those sick persons whose term of life had arrived, it could not be found. Thus, on the very day on which King Brude died, though it was sought for, yet it could not be found in the place where it had been previously laid.

CHAPTER XXXV.

Of the manner in which St. Columba overcame Broichan the Druid
and sailed against the wind.

On a certain day after the events recorded in the foregoing
chapters, Broichan, whilst conversing with the saint, said to
him : " Tell me, Columba, when dost thou propose to set sail ? "
The saint replied, " I intend to begin my voyage after three
days, if God permits me, and preserves my life." Broichan said,
" On the contrary, thou shalt not be able, for I can make the
winds unfavourable to thy voyage, and cause a great darkness
to envelop you in its shade." Upon this the saint observed :
" The almighty power of God ruleth all things, and in His name
and under His guiding providence all our movements are
directed." What more need I say ? That same day, the saint,
accompanied by a large number of followers, went to the long
lake of the river Nesa (Loch Ness), as he had determined. Then
the Druids began to exult, seeing that it had become very dark,
and that the wind was very violent and contrary. Nor should
we wonder, that God sometimes allows them, with the aid of evil
spirits, to raise tempests and agitate the sea. For thus legions
of demons once met in the midst of the sea the holy bishop
Germanus, whilst on his voyage through the Gallican channel
to Britain, whither he was going from zeal for the salvation of
souls, and exposed him to great dangers, by raising a violent
storm and causing great darkness whilst it was yet day. But
all these things were dissipated by the prayers of St. Germanus more rapidly than his words were uttered, and the darkness passed away.

Our Columba, therefore, seeing that the sea was violently
agitated, and that the wind was most unfavourable for his voyage, called on Christ the Lord and embarked in his small boat ;
and whilst the sailors hesitated, he the more confidently ordered
them to raise the sails against the wind. No sooner was this
order executed, while the whole crowd was looking on, than the
vessel ran against the wind with extraordinary speed. And
after a short time, the wind, which hitherto had been against
them, veered round to help them on their voyage, to the intense
astonishment of all. And thus throughout the remainder of that
day the light breeze continued most favourable, and the skiff of
blessed man was carried safely to the wished-for haven.

Let the reader therefore consider how great and eminent this
venerable man must have been, upon whom God Almighty, for

the purpose of manifesting His illustrious name before a heathen people, bestowed the gift of working such miracles as those we have recorded.

CHAPTER XXXVI.

Of the sudden opening of the door of the Royal Fortress of its own accord.

At another time, when the saint made his first journey to King Brude, it happened that the king, elated by the pride of royalty, acted haughtily, and would not open his gates on the first arrival of the blessed man. When the man of God observed this, he approached the folding doors with his companions, and having first formed upon them the sign of the cross of our Lord, he then knocked at and laid his hand upon the gate, which instantly flew open of its own accord, the bolts having been driven back with great force. The saint and his companions then passed through the gate thus speedily opened. And when the king learned what had occurred, he and his councillors were filled with alarm, and immediately setting out from the palace, he advanced to meet with due respect the blessed man, whom he addressed in the most conciliating and respectful language. And ever after from that day, so long as he lived, the king held this holy and reverend man in very great honour, as was due.

CHAPTER XXXVII.

Of a similar unclosing of the Church of the Field of the Two Streams (Tirdaglas, in the county of Tipperary).

Upon another occasion, when the saint was staying a few days in Scotia (Ireland), he went, on invitation, to visit the brethren in the monastery of the Field of the Two Streams (Tirdaglas). But it happened, by some accident, that when he arrived at the church the keys of the oratory could not be found. When the saint observed the brethren lamenting to one another about the keys being astray, and the door locked, he went himself to the door and said, "The Lord is able, without a key, to open his own house for his servants." At these words, the bolts of the lock were driven back with great force, and the door opened of itself. The saint entered the church before all with universal admiration; and he was afterwards most hospitably entertained by the brethren, and treated by all with the greatest respect and veneration.

CHAPTER XXXVIII.

Concerning a certain Peasant who was a beggar, for whom the Saint made and blessed a stake for killing wild beasts.

AT another time there came to St. Columba a very poor peasant, who lived in the district which borders the shores of the Aporic lake (Lochaber). The blessed man, taking pity on the wretched man, who had not wherewithal to support his wife and family, gave him all the alms he could afford, and then said to him, " Poor man, take a branch from the neighbouring wood, and bring it to me quickly." The wretched man brought the branch as he was directed, and the saint, taking it in his own hand, sharpened it to a point like a stake, and, blessing it, gave it back to the destitute man, saying, " Preserve this stake with great care, and it, I believe, will never hurt men or cattle, but only wild beasts and fishes; and as long as thou preservest this stake thou shalt never be without abundance of venison in thy house."

The wretched beggar upon hearing this was greatly delighted, and returning home, fixed the stake in a remote place which was frequented by the wild beasts of the forest; and when that next night was past, he went at early morning dawn to see the stake, and found a stag of great size that had fallen upon it and been transfixed by it. Why should I mention more instances? Not a day could pass, so the tradition goes, in which he did not find a stag or hind or some other wild beast fixed upon the stake; and his whole house being thus filled with the flesh of the wild beasts, he sold to his neighbours all that remained after his own family was supplied. But, as in the case of Adam, the envy of the devil also found out this miserable man also through his wife, who, not as a prudent matron, but rather like one infatuated, thus spoke to her husband: " Remove the stake out of the earth, for if men, or cattle, perish on it, then thou and I and our children shall be put to death, or led into captivity." To these words her husband replied, " It will not be so, for when the holy man blessed the stake he said it would never injure men or cattle." Still the miserable man, after saying this, yielded to his wife, and taking the stake out of the earth, like a man deprived of his reason, brought it into the house and placed it against the wall. Soon after his house-dog

fell upon it and was killed, and on its death his wife said to
him, "One of thy children will fall upon it and be killed." At
these words of his wife he removed the stake out of the house,
and having carried it to a forest, placed it in the thickest brush-
wood, where, as he thought, no animal could be hurt by it; but
upon his return the following day he found a roe had fallen
upon it and perished. He then took it away and concealed it
by thrusting it under the water in the edge of the river, which
may be called in Latin Nigra Dea (not identified). On returning
the next day he found transfixed, and still held by it, a salmon
of extraordinary size, which he was scarcely able by himself to
take from the river and carry home. At the same time, he
took the stake again back with him from the water, and placed
it outside on the top of his house, where a crow having soon
after lighted, was instantly killed by the force of the fall.
Upon this the miserable man, yielding again to the advice of
his foolish wife, took down the stake from the house-top, and
taking an axe cut it in many pieces, and threw them into the fire.
Having thus deprived himself of this effectual means of alle-
viating his distress, he was again, as he deserved to be, reduced
to beggary. This freedom from want was owing to the stake,
so frequently mentioned above, which the blessed man had
blest and given him, and which, so long as it was kept, could
suffice for snares and nets, and every kind of fishing and
hunting; but when the stake was lost, the wretched peasant,
though he had been enriched for the time, could only, when too
late, lament over it with his whole family all the rest of his
life.

CHAPTER XXXIX.

*Concerning a Leathern Vessel for holding milk which was carried
from its place by the ebb, and brought back again by the
return of the tide.*

On another occasion, when the blessed man's messenger, who
was named Lugaid, and surnamed Laitir, was at his command
making preparations for a voyage to Scotia (Ireland), he searched
for and found amongst the sea-going articles that belonged to
the saint's ship a leathern vessel for holding milk. This vessel he
immersed in the sea in order to moisten it, and put upon it stones
of considerable size. He then went to the saint, and told him
what he had done with the leathern bottle. The saint smiled
and said, "I do not think that this vessel, which thou sayest
thou hast sunk under the waves, will accompany thee to Hibernia

on the present occasion." "Why," rejoined Lugaid, "can I not take it with me in the ship?" The saint replied, "Thou shalt learn the reason to-morrow, as the event will prove."

On the following morning, therefore, Lugaid went to take the vessel out of the sea, but the ebb of the tide had carried it away during the night. When he could not find it, he returned in grief to the saint, and on his bended knees on the ground confessed his negligence. St. Columba consoled him, saying, "My brother, grieve not for perishable things. The vessel which the ebbing tide has carried away the returning tide will, after your departure, bring back to the spot where thou didst place it." At the ninth hour of the same day, soon after the departure of Lugaid from the Iouan island (Hy, now Iona), the saint addressed those who stood near him, and said, "Let one of you now go to the sea, for the leathern vessel for which Lugaid was lamenting, when it was carried away by the ebbing tide, hath been brought back by the returning tide, and is to be found at the place from which it was taken." Upon hearing these words spoken by the saint, a certain active youth ran to the sea-shore, where he found the vessel, as the saint had predicted. He immediately took it out of the water, and with great joy hastened back at full speed to the holy man, into whose hands he delivered it, amid the great admiration of all the beholders.

In the two miracles which we have just recorded, and which regard such common and trifling things as a wooden stake and a leathern vessel, there may, nevertheless, be observed, as we noticed before, the gift of prophecy united with the power of working miracles.

Let us now proceed with our narrative regarding other things.

CHAPTER XL.

The Saint's prophecy regarding Libran, of the Rush-ground.

AT another time, while the saint was living in the Iouan island (Hy, now Iona), a certain man of humble birth, who had lately assumed the clerical habit, sailed over from Scotia (Ireland), and came to the blessed man's monastery on the island. The saint found him one day sitting alone in the lodging provided for strangers, and inquired first about his country, family, and the object of his journey. He replied that he was born in the region of the Connacht men (Connaught), and that he had undertaken that long and weary journey to

atone for his sins by the pilgrimage.   In order to test the depth
of his repentance, the saint then laid down minutely before his
eyes the hardship and labour attending the monastic exercises.
" I am prepared," he replied at once to the saint, "to do everything whatever thou dost bid me, however hard and however
humiliating."   Why add more ?   That same hour he confessed
all his sins, and promised, kneeling on the ground, to fulfil the
laws of penance.   The saint said to him, " Arise and take a seat."
Then he thus addressed him as he sat, " Thou must do penance
for seven years in the Ethican land (Tiree); thou and I, with
God's blessing, shall survive that period of seven years."   Being
comforted by the saint's words, he first gave thanks to God, and
turning afterwards to the saint, asked, " What am I to do with
regard to an oath which I have violated ? for while living in my
own country I murdered a certain man, and afterwards, as guilty
of murdering him, I was confined in prison.   But a certain very
wealthy blood-relation came to my aid, and promptly loosing
me from my prison-chains, rescued me from the death to which
I was condemned.   When I was released, I bound myself by
oath to serve that friend all the days of my life; but I had
remained only a short time in his service, when I felt ashamed
of serving man, and very much preferred to devote myself to
God.   I therefore left that earthly master, broke the oath, and
departing, reached thee safely, God prospering my journey thus
far."   The saint, on seeing him very much grieved over such
things, and first prophesying with respect to him, thus made
answer, saying, " At the end of seven years, as I said to thee,
thou shalt come to me here during the forty days of Lent, and
thou shalt approach the altar and partake of the Eucharist at
the great Paschal festival."   Why hang longer over words ?
The penitent stranger in every respect obeyed the saint's commands; and being sent at that time to the monastery of the
Plain of Lunge (Magh Lunge, in Tiree), and having fully completed his seven years' penance there, returned to him during
Lent, according to the previous command and prophecy.   After
celebrating the Paschal solemnity, and coming at that time to
the altar as directed, he came again to the saint to consult him
on the above-mentioned oath.   Then the saint gave this prophetic
answer to his inquiry, " That earthly master of thine of whom
thou hast formerly spoken is still living; so are thy father, thy
mother, and thy brethren.   Thou must now, therefore, prepare
thyself for the voyage."   And while speaking, he drew forth a
sword ornamented with carved ivory, and said, " Take this gift
to carry with thee, and offer it to thy master as the price of
thy ransom ; but when thou dost, he will on no account accept

it, for he has a virtuous, kindly-disposed wife, and by the influence of her wholesome counsel he shall that very day, without recompense or ransom, set thee free, unbinding the girdle round thy captive loins. But though thus relieved from this anxiety, thou shalt not escape a source of disquietude arising on another hand, for thy brethren will come round and press thee to make good the support due to thy father for so long a time which thou hast neglected. Comply thou at once with their wish, and take in hand dutifully to cherish thine aged father. Though the duty may, indeed, seem weighty, thou must not be grieved thereat, because thou shalt soon be relieved of it; for from the day on which thou shalt take charge of thy father, the end of that same week shall see his death and burial. But after thy father's burial thy brethren will a second time come and sharply demand of thee that thou pay the expenses due for thy mother. However, thy younger brother will assuredly set thee free from this necessity by engaging to perform in thy stead every duty or obligation which thou owest to thy mother."

Having heard these words, the above-mentioned brother, whose name was Libran, received the gift, and set out enriched with the saint's blessing. When he reached his native country, he found everything exactly as prophesied by the saint. For when he showed and made offer of the price of his freedom to his master, his wife opposed his wish to accept it, saying, "What need have we to accept this ransom sent by St. Columba? We are not even worthy of such a favour. Release this dutiful servant without payment. The prayers of the holy man will profit us more than this price which is offered us." The husband, therefore, listening to his wife's wholesome counsel, set the slave free at once without ransom. He was afterwards, according to the saint's prophecy, compelled by his brethren to undertake the providing for his father, and he buried him at his death on the seventh day. After his burial they required him to discharge the same duty to his mother; but a younger brother, as the saint foretold, engaged to supply his place, and thus released him from the obligation. "We ought not on any account," said he to his brethren, "detain this our brother at home, who, for the salvation of his soul, has spent seven years in penitential exercises with St. Columba in Britain."

After being thus released from the matters which gave him annoyance, he bade farewell to his mother and brothers, and returned a free man to a place called in the Scotic tongue Daire Calgaich (Derry). There he found a ship under sail just leaving the harbour, and he called to the sailors to take him on board and convey him to Britain. But they, not being the monks of St. Columba, refused to receive him. He then prayed to the venerable man, who, though far distant, indeed, in body, yet was present in spirit, as the event soon proved, saying, "Is it thy will, holy Columba, that these sailors, who do not receive me, thy companion, proceed upon their voyage with full sails and favourable winds?"

At this saying the wind, which till then was favourable for them, veered round on the instant to the opposite point. While this was taking place, the sailors saw again the same man running in a line with them along the bank of the river, and, hastily taking counsel together, they cried out to him from the ship, saying, "Perhaps the wind hath suddenly turned against us, for this reason, that we refused to give thee a passage; but if even now we were to invite thee to be with us on board, couldst thou change these contrary winds to be in our favour?" When the pilgrim heard this, he said to them, "St. Columba, to whom I am going, and whom I have served for the last seven years, is able by prayer, if you take me on board, to obtain a favourable wind for you from his Lord." They then, on hearing this, approached the land with their ship, and asked him to join them in it. As soon as he came on board, he said, "In the name of the Almighty God, whom St. Columba blamelessly serveth, spread your sails on the extended yards." And when they had done so, the gale of contrary winds immediately became favourable, and the vessel made a prosperous voyage under full sail to Britain. After reaching the shores of Britain, Libran left the ship, blessed the sailors, and went directly to St. Columba, who was staying in the Iouan island (Hy, now Iona). The blessed man welcomed him with joy, and, without receiving the information from any one, told him fully of everything that happened on his way—of his master and the wife's kindly suggestion, and of his being set free by her advice; of his brethren also, and the death and burial of his father within the week; of his mother, and the timely assistance of the younger brother; of what occurred as he was returning, the adverse and favourable winds; of the words of the sailors when first they refused to take him in; of the promise of fair wind, and of the favourable change when they took him on board their vessel. Why need I add more? Every particular the saint foretold he now described after it was exactly fulfilled.

After these words, the traveller gave back to the saint the price of his ransom which he had received from him; and at the same time the saint addressed him in these words: "Inasmuch as thou art free, thou shalt be called Libran." Libran took at the same period the monastic vows with much fervour. And when he was being sent back again by the holy man to the monastery where he had formerly served the Lord during the seven years of penance, he received in farewell the following prophetic announcement regarding himself:—"Thou shalt live yet a long time, and end this present life in a good old age; yet thou shalt not arise from the dead in Britain, but in Scotia (Ireland)." Hearing these words, he knelt down and wept bitterly. When the saint saw his great grief he tried to comfort him, saying, "Arise, and be not sad.   Thou shalt die in one of my monasteries, and thy lot shall be among my chosen monks in the kingdom; and with them thou shalt awake from the sleep of death unto the resurrection of life."   When he heard this unusual consolation from the saint he rejoiced exceedingly, and, being enriched by the saint's blessing, went away in peace. This truthful prophecy of the saint regarding the same man was afterwards fulfilled; for when he had faithfully served the Lord for many revolving years of holy obedience in the monastery of the Plain of Lunge (Magh Lunge, in Tiree), after the departure of St. Columba from the world, he was sent, in extreme old age, on a mission to Scotia regarding the interests of the monastery, and proceeded as soon as he landed through the Plain of Breg (Maghbreg, in Meath), till he reached the monastery of the Oak-wood Plain (Derry).   Being there received as a stranger in the guest-chamber, and suffering from a certain disease, he passed to the Lord in peace on the seventh day of his illness, and was buried with the chosen monks of St. Columba, according to his prophecy, to await the resurrection unto eternal life.

Let it suffice that we have written these truthful prophecies of St. Columba regarding Libran of the Rush-ground.   He was called " of the Rush-ground " from his having been engaged many years in the labour of collecting rushes.

CHAPTER XLI.

Concerning a certain little Woman who, as a daughter of Eve, was enduring the great and extremely dangerous pains of Childbirth.

ON a certain day during the saint's stay in the Iouan island (Hy, now Iona), the saint arose from reading, and said with a smile, "I must now hasten to the oratory to pray to the Lord on behalf of a poor woman in Hibernia, who at this moment is suffering the pangs of a most difficult childbirth, and is calling upon the name of Columba. She trusteth that God will grant her relief from her sufferings through my prayers, because she is a relation of mine, being lineally descended from the house of my mother's parentage."

Having said this, the saint, being touched with pity for the poor woman, hastened to the church, and, on his bended knees, earnestly prayed for her to Christ, who was Himself by birth a partaker of humanity. Returning from the church after his prayer, he said to the brethren who met him, "The Lord Jesus, born of a woman, hath given seasonable help to this poor woman, and hath mercifully relieved her from her distress. She hath been safely delivered of a child, nor shall she die upon this occasion." That same hour, as the saint had predicted, the poor woman, by invoking his name, was safely delivered, and restored to perfect health, as we afterwards learned from travellers who came to us from that part of Scotia (Ireland) where the woman resided.

CHAPTER XLII.

Of one Lugne, surnamed Tudida, a Pilot, who lived on the Rech-rean island (either Rathlin or Lambay), and whom, as being deformed, his wife hated.

ANOTHER time, when the saint was living on the Rechrean island, a certain man of humble birth came to him and complained of his wife, who, as he said, so hated him, that she would on no account allow him to come near her for marriage rights. The saint on hearing this, sent for the wife, and, so far as he could, began to reprove her on that account, saying: "Why, O woman, dost thou endeavour to withdraw thy flesh from thyself, while the Lord says, 'They shall be two in one flesh'? Wherefore the flesh of thy husband is thy flesh." She answered and said, "Whatever thou shalt require of me I am ready to do, however hard it may be, with this single exception, that thou dost not urge me in any way to sleep in one bed with Lugne. I do not refuse to perform every duty at home, or, if thou dost command me, even to pass over the seas, or to live in some monastery for women." The saint then said, "What thou dost propose cannot be lawfully done, for thou art bound by the law of the husband as long as thy husband liveth, for it would be impious to separate those whom God has lawfully joined together." Immediately after these words he added: "This day let us three, namely, the husband and his wife and myself, join

in prayer to the Lord and in fasting." But the woman replied :
" I know it is not impossible for thee to obtain from God, when
thou askest them, those things that seem to us either difficult, or
even impossible." It is unnecessary to say more. The husband
and wife agreed to fast with the saint that day, and the following night the saint spent sleepless in prayer for them. Next
day he thus addressed the wife in presence of her husband, and
said to her : " O woman, art thou still ready to-day, as thou saidst
yesterday, to go away to a convent of women ?" "I know
now," she answered, " that thy prayer to God for me hath been
heard ; for that man whom I hated yesterday, I love to-day ; for
my heart hath been changed last night in some unknown way—
from hatred to love." Why need we linger over it ? From that
day to the hour of death, the soul of the wife was firmly
cemented in affection to her husband, so that she no longer
refused those mutual matrimonial rights which she was formerly
unwilling to allow.

CHAPTER XLIII.

The Prophecy of the blessed man regarding the Voyage of Cormac
the grandson of Lethan.

AT another time a soldier of Christ, named Cormac, about
whom we have related a few brief particulars in the first part of
this book, made even a second attempt to discover a desert in
the ocean. After he had gone far from the land over the
boundless ocean at full sail, St. Columba, who was then staying
beyond the Dorsal Ridge of Britain (Drumalban), recommended
him in the following terms to King Brude, in the presence of the
ruler of the Orcades (Orkneys): " Some of our brethren have
lately set sail, and are anxious to discover a desert in the path-
less sea ; should they happen, after many wanderings, to come
to the Orcadian islands, do thou carefully instruct this chief,
whose hostages are in thy hand, that no evil befall them within
his dominions." The saint took care to give this direction, because he knew that after a few months Cormac would arrive at
the Orcades. So it afterwards came to pass, and to this advice
of the holy man Cormac owed his escape from impending death.
After the lapse of a few months, whilst the saint was remaining in the Iouan island (Hy, now Iona), Cormac's name was
mentioned one day unexpectedly in his presence by some persons in conversation, who were observing that it was not yet
known whether the voyage of Cormac had been successful or

otherwise.   Upon hearing this, the saint joined the conversation and said : " You shall see Cormac, about whom you are
now speaking, arrive here to-day."

And after about an hour, wonderful to relate, lo ! Cormac
unexpectedly arrived, and proceeded to the oratory whilst all
expressed their admiration and gave thanks to God.

Having mentioned thus briefly the prediction of the blessed
man regarding Cormac's second voyage, we have now to relate
another equally remarkable instance of the holy man's prophetic
knowledge regarding his third voyage.

When Cormac was laboriously engaged in his third voyage
over the ocean, he was exposed to the most imminent danger
of death.   For, when for fourteen days in summer, and as many
nights, his vessel sailed with full sails before a south wind, in a
straight course from land, into the northern regions, his voyage
seemed to be extended beyond the limits of human wanderings,
and return to be impossible.

Accordingly, after the tenth hour of the fourteenth day, certain dangers of a most formidable and almost insurmountable
kind presented themselves.   A multitude of loathsome and
annoying insects, such as had never been seen before, covered
the sea in swarms, and struck the keel and sides, the prow, and
stern of the vessel, so very violently, that it seemed as if they
would wholly penetrate the leathern covering of the ship.   According to the accounts afterwards given by those who were
there, they were about the size of frogs ; they could swim, but
were not able to fly ; their sting was extremely painful, and
they crowded upon the handles of the oars.

When Cormac and his fellow-voyagers had seen these and
other monsters, which it is not now our province to describe,
they were filled with fear and alarm, and, shedding copious
tears, they prayed to God, who is a kind and ready helper of
those who are in trouble.   At that same hour our holy Columba,
although far away in body, was present in spirit with Cormac
in the ship.   Accordingly he gave the signal, and calling the
brethren to the oratory, he entered the church, and addressing
those who were present, he uttered the following prophecy in
his usual manner : " Brethren, pray with all your usual fervour
for Cormac, who by sailing too far hath passed the bounds of
human enterprise, and is exposed at this moment to dreadful
alarm and fright, in the presence of monsters which were never
before seen, and are almost indescribable.   We ought, therefore,
to sympathize with our brethren and associates who are in such
imminent danger, and to pray to the Lord with them ; behold
at this moment Cormac and his sailors are shedding copious

tears, and praying with intense fervency to Christ; let us assist them by our prayers, that God may take compassion upon us, and cause the wind, which for the past fourteen days has blown from the south, to blow from the north, and this north wind will, of course, deliver Cormac's vessel out of all danger."

Having said this he knelt before the altar, and in a plaintive voice poured forth his prayers to the almighty power of God, who governeth the winds and all things. After having prayed he arose quickly, and wiping away his tears, joyfully gave thanks to God, saying, "Now, brethren, let us congratulate our dear friends for whom we have been praying, for God will now change the south into a north wind, which will free our associates from their perils, and bring them to us here again." As he spoke the south wind ceased, and a north wind blew for many days after, so that Cormac's ship was enabled to gain the land. And Cormac hastened to visit Columba, and in God's bounty they looked on each other again face to face, to the extreme joy and wonder of all. Let the reader, then, carefully consider how great and of what a character the blessed man must have been, who possessed such prophetic knowledge, and who, by invoking the name of Christ, could rule the winds and the waves.

CHAPTER XLIV.

How the venerable man made a Journey in a Chariot which was not secured with the proper linch-pins.

AT another time, while the saint was spending a few days in Scotia (Ireland), some ecclesiastical object required his presence, and accordingly he ascended a yoked car which he had previously blessed ; but from some unaccountable neglect the requisite linch-pins were not inserted in the holes at the extremities of the axles. The person who on this occasion performed the duty of driver in the carriage with St. Columba was Columban, a holy man, the son of Echud, and founder of that monastery which is called in the Scotic language Snam luthir (now Slanore, in Granard, county of Longford). The distance they rode that day was very long, and the jolting severe, yet the wheels did not come off the axles nor even stir from their proper places, although, as was mentioned before, there were no linch-pins to secure them. But divine grace alone so favoured the venerable man that the car in which he was safely seated proceeded without being upset, or meeting any obstacle to retard its progress.

Thus far we may have written enough regarding the miracles which the divine omnipotence wrought through this remarkable man while he lived; we shall now mention also a few out of many well-authenticated miracles which the Lord was pleased to grant to him after his death.

CHAPTER XLV.

Of the Rain which, after some months of drought, the Lord boun-
tifully poured out upon the earth in honour of the blessed
man.

ABOUT fourteen years before the date at which we write, there occurred during the spring a very great and long-continued drought in these marshy regions, insomuch that the threat denounced against sinners in the Book of Leviticus seemed to impend over the people : " I will give to you the heaven above as iron, and the earth as brass.   Your labour shall be spent in vain, the ground shall not bring forth her increase, nor the trees their fruit," etc.

We therefore, reading these words, and fearing the impend-ing calamity, took counsel together, and resolved that some of the senior members of the community should walk round a newly ploughed and sowed field, taking with them the white tunic of St. Columba, and some books written in his own hand, that they should raise in the air, and shake three times the tunic which the saint wore at the hour of his death ; and that they then should open the books and read them on the little hill of the angels (now called Sithean Mor), where the citizens of the heavenly country were occasionally seen to descend at the bidding of the blessed man.   When these directions had been executed in the manner prescribed, then, strange to relate, the sky, which during the preceding months of March and April had been cloudless, was suddenly covered with dense vapours that arose from the sea with extraordinary rapidity; copious rain fell day and night, and the parched earth being sufficiently moistened, produced its fruits in good season, and yielded the same year a most abundant harvest.   And thus the invocation of the very name of the blessed man, by the exhibition of his tunic and books, obtained seasonable relief at the same time for many places and much people.

CHAPTER XLVI.

Of the unfavourable Winds which, through the intercession of our Saint, were changed into propitious breezes.

OUR belief in the miracles which we have recorded, but which we did not ourselves see, is confirmed beyond doubt by the miracles of which we were eye-witnesses; for on three different occasions we saw unfavourable gales of wind changed unto propitious breezes.

On the first occasion we had to draw over land long boats of hewn pine and oak, and to bring home in the same way a large quantity of materials for building ships. In order to obtain from the Lord a favourable wind for our voyage, we took counsel and put the books and garments of the blessed man upon the altar, and at the same time fasted, chanted psalms, and invoked his name. And this was granted to the holy man by God's favour, for on the day that our sailors had made all their preparations, and were ready to convey the wood for the purposes above mentioned in curachs and skiffs, the wind, which for several days before had been contrary, suddenly changed into favourable breezes. They blew steadily the entire day, by God's blessing, and enabled the whole fleet of boats to make their long and dangerous passage to the Iouan island (Hy, now Iona), with safety and expedition.

On the second occasion, which was a few years after the one just mentioned, our monastery was requiring repairs, and some oak-trees were to be taken from near the mouth of the river Sale (the Seil, in Lorn), in twelve vessels which we brought for the purpose. Our sailors then rowed out to sea with their oars, the day being calm and the sea tranquil, when suddenly a westerly wind, which is also called Zephyr, sprang up, and we betook ourselves to the nearest island, which is called in Scotic Airthrago (probably Kerrera), to seek for shelter in a harbour in it.

But in the meantime we began to complain of this unfavourable change in the wind, and in some measure even to blame our Columba, saying, "Doth our unfortunate detention in this place please thee, O saint? Hitherto we had hoped that we might receive from thee some aid and comfort in our labours through the divine favour, seeing we thought that thou wert honoured and powerful in the sight of God."

No sooner had we thus spoken, than, wonderful to relate,

the unfavourable west wind ceased, and immediately, in the course as it were of one minute, behold a most favourable south-eastern breeze sprang up. The sailors were then directed to raise the sail yards in the form of a cross, and spread the sails upon them; thus putting to sea with a steady and favourable breeze, we were enabled, without the slightest fatigue, to reach our island that same day, rejoicing in our cargo of wood, and in the company of all who were engaged in assisting us in the ships. Thus the chiding with the holy man, slight though it was, in that complaint assisted us not a little; and in what and how great esteem the saint is held by the Lord is evident from His hearing him so quickly and changing the winds.

Then the third instance was in the summer, after the celebration of a synod in Hibernia, when we were detained by contrary winds for a few days among the people of the tribe of Loern (Lorn), and had reached the Sainean island (Shuna). There the vigil and the feast of St. Columba found us extremely sad and disconsolate, because we wished to celebrate that joyous day in the Iouan island (Hy, now Iona). Accordingly, as on a former occasion, we began to complain and to say, " Is it agreeable to thee, O saint, that we should spend to-morrow, thy festival-day, among strangers, and not celebrate it in thine own church? It is easy for thee in the morning of such a day to obtain from the Lord that the contrary winds may become favourable, and that we may be able to celebrate the solemn mass of thy birth in thine own church. On the following morning we arose at daybreak, and seeing that the adverse winds had ceased, we went on board our vessels and put to sea in a profound calm, when, lo! there suddenly sprung up a south wind, which was most favourable for the voyage. The sailors then joyously raised the sails, and on this occasion also without any exertion on our part, so quick and so favourable was our passage, owing to the mercy of God to the blessed man, that we reached the landing-place of the Iouan island (Hy, now Iona), after the third hour, according to our previous anxious desire. After washing our hands and feet we entered the church at the sixth hour in company with our brethren, and celebrated at once the holy services of the mass of St. Columba and St. Baithene, whose festivals occurred on that day, at the daybreak of which, as we said above, we started from the distant Sainean island (Shuna).

And as to the truth of this story I have now related, there are yet living, not merely one or two witnesses as the law requires, but hundreds and more who can bear testimony.

CHAPTER XLVII.

Concerning the Plague.

WHAT we are about to relate concerning the plague, which in our own time twice visited the greater part of the world, deserves, I think, to be reckoned among not the least of the miracles of St. Columba. For, not to mention the other and greater countries of Europe, including Italy, the Roman States, and the Cisalpine provinces of Gaul, with the States of Spain also, which lie beyond the Pyrenees, these islands of the sea, Scotia (Ireland) and Britain, have twice been ravaged by a dreadful pestilence throughout their whole extent, except among the two tribes, the Picts and Scots of Britain, who are separated from each other by the Dorsal mountains of Britain. And although neither of these nations was free from those grievous crimes which generally provoke the anger of the eternal Judge, yet both have been hitherto patiently borne with and mercifully spared. Now, to what other person can this favour granted them by God be attributed unless to St. Columba, whose monasteries lie within the territories of both these people, and have been regarded by both with the greatest respect up to the present time? But what I am now to say cannot, I think, be heard without a sigh, that there are many very stupid people in both countries who, in their ignorance that they owe their exemption from the plague to the prayers of the saint, ungratefully and wickedly abuse the patience and the goodness of God. But I often return my most grateful thanks to God for having, through the intercession of our holy patron, preserved me and those in our islands from the ravages of the pestilence; and that in Saxonia also, when I went to visit my friend King Aldfrid, where the plague was raging and laying waste many of his villages, yet both in its first attack, immediately after the war of Ecfridus, and in its second, two years subsequently, the Lord mercifully saved me from danger, though I was living and moving about in the very midst of the plague. The Divine mercy was also extended to my companions, not one of whom died of the plague, or was attacked with any other disease.

Here must end the second Book recording the miracles, and it is right for me to draw attention to the fact, that many well-authenticated miracles have been omitted in order not to fatigue the reader.

Here endeth the Second Book.

BOOK III.

HERE BEGINNETH THE THIRD BOOK.

OF THE VISIONS OF ANGELS.

CHAPTER I.

IN the first of these three little Books we have, under the guidance of God, shortly and concisely related, as was observed before, some of the prophetic revelations. In the second we have recorded the powerful miracles the blessed man wrought, which, as we have often observed, were generally accompanied with the gift of prophecy. But in this third Book, which treateth of the Apparitions of Angels, we shall relate those which either our saint received regarding others, or others saw regarding him ; we shall also describe some which were manifested to both parties, though in different measure, that is, to the saint himself, specially and clearly, but to the others improperly and partially, or, in other words, externally and tentatively, yet in the same visions either of angels, or of heavenly light. Whatever discrepancies however in any case may at first sight seem to occur in those visions, will be completely removed as we proceed to relate them in their proper places. But now we must begin at the very birth of the blessed man, and relate these angelic manifestations.

CHAPTER II.

ON a certain night between the conception and birth of the venerable man, an angel of the Lord appeared to his mother in dreams, bringing to her, as he stood by her, a certain robe of extraordinary beauty, in which the most beautiful colours, as it were, of all the flowers seemed to be portrayed. After a short time he asked it back, and took it out of her hands, and having raised it and spread it out, he let it fly through the air. But she being sad at the loss of it, said to that man of venerable aspect, "Why dost thou take this lovely cloak away from me so soon?" He immediately replied, "Because this mantle is so exceedingly honourable that thou canst not retain it longer with thee." When this was said, the woman saw that the fore-mentioned robe was gradually receding from her in its flight; and that then it expanded until its width exceeded the plains, and in all its measurements was larger than the mountains and forests. Then she heard the following words: "Woman, do not grieve, for to the man to whom thou hast been joined by the marriage bond, thou shalt bring forth a son, of so beautiful a character, that he shall be reckoned among his own people as one of the prophets of God, and hath been predestined by God to be the leader of innumerable souls to the heavenly country." At these words the woman awoke from her sleep.

CHAPTER III.

Of the Ray of Light which was seen upon the boy's face as he lay asleep.

On another night, Cruithnecan, a priest of blameless life, to whose care the blessed youth was confided, upon returning home from the church after mass, found his house illuminated with a bright light, and saw in fact a ball of fire standing over the face of the little boy as he lay asleep. At the sight he at once shook with fear, and fell down with his face to the ground in great amazement, well knowing that it indicated the grace of the Holy Spirit poured out from heaven upon his young charge.

CHAPTER IV.

Of the Apparition of Holy Angels whom St. Brenden saw accompanying the blessed man through the plain.

For indeed after the lapse of many years, when St. Columba was excommunicated by a certain synod for some pardonable and very trifling reasons, and indeed unjustly, as it afterwards appeared at the end, he came to the same meeting convened against himself. When St. Brenden, the founder of the monastery which in the Scotic language is called Birra (Birr, in King's County), saw him approaching in the distance, he quickly arose, and with head bowed down reverently kissed him. When some of the seniors in that assembly, going apart from the rest, were finding fault with him, and saying : " Why didst thou not decline to rise in presence of an excommunicated person, and to kiss him ?" he replied to them in this wise : " If," said he, " you had seen what the Lord has this day thought fit to show to me regarding this his chosen one, whom you dishonour, you would never have excommunicated a person whom God not only doth not excommunicate, according to your unjust sentence, but even more and more highly esteemeth." " How, we would wish to know," said they in reply, " doth God exalt, as thou sayest, on whom we have excommunicated, not without reason ? " " I have seen," said Brenden, " a most brilliant pillar wreathed with fiery tresses preceding this same man of God whom you treat with contempt ; I have also seen holy angels accompanying him on his journey through the plain. Therefore I do not dare to slight him whom I see foreordained by God to be the leader of his people to life." When he said this, they desisted, and so far from daring to hold the saint any longer excommunicated, they even treated him with the greatest respect and reverence. This took place in Teilte (Taillte, now Teltown, in Meath).

CHAPTER V.

Of the Angel of the Lord which St. Finnio saw accompanying the blessed man in his journey.

ON another occasion the holy man went to the venerable Bishop Finnio, who had formerly been his preceptor,—the youth to visit the man far advanced in years. When St. Finnio saw him coming to him, he observed also an angel of the Lord accompanying him, as he proceeded, and as it is handed down to us by well-informed persons, he made it known to certain brethren who were standing by, saying to them : " Behold, look now to Columba as he draweth near; he hath been deemed worthy of having an angelic inhabitant of heaven to be his companion in his wanderings." About that same time the holy man, with his twelve disciples and fellow-soldiers, sailed across to Britain.

CHAPTER VI.

How an Angel of the Lord appeared in a vision to St. Columba while he stayed in the Hinba island (Eilean-na-Naoimh), being sent to him in order that he might appoint Aidan king.

ON another occasion, when this eminent man was staying in the Hinba island (Eilean-na-Naoimh), he saw, on a certain night, in a mental ecstasy, an angel sent to him from heaven, and holding in his hand a book of glass, regarding the appointment of kings. Having received the book from the hand of the angel, the venerable man, at his command, began to read it; and when he was reluctant to appoint Aidan king, as the book directed, because he had a greater affection for Iogenan his brother, the angel, suddenly stretching forth his hand, struck the saint with a scourge, the livid marks of which remained in his side all the days of his life. And he added these words: "Know for certain," said he, "that I am sent to thee by God with the book of glass, that in accordance with the words thou hast read therein, thou mayest inaugurate Aidan into the kingdom; but if thou refuse to obey this command, I will strike thee again." When therefore this angel of the Lord had appeared for three successive nights, having the same book of glass in his hand, and had repeated the same commands of the Lord regarding the appointment of the same king, the saint, in obedience to the command of the Lord, sailed across to the Iouan island (Hy, now Iona), and there ordained, as he had been commanded, Aidan to be king, who had arrived at the same time as the saint. During the words of consecration, the saint declared the future regarding the children, grandchildren, and great-grandchildren of Aidan, and laying his hand upon his head, he consecrated and blessed him.

Cummene the Fair, in the book which he wrote on the virtues of St. Columba, states that St. Columba commenced his predictions regarding Aidan and his children and kingdom in the following manner: "Believe me, unhesitatingly, O Aidan," said he, "none of thine enemies shall be able to resist thee, unless thou first act unjustly towards me and my successors. Wherefore direct thou thy children to commend to their children, their grandchildren, and their posterity, not to let the sceptre pass out of their hands through evil counsels. For at whatever time they turn against me or my relatives who are in

Hibernia, the scourge which I suffered on thy account from the angel shall bring great disgrace upon them by the hand of God, and the hearts of men shall be turned away from them, and their foes shall be greatly strengthened against them." Now this prophecy hath been fulfilled in our own times in the battle of Roth (Magh Rath, fought 637), in which Domnall Brecc, the grandson of Aidan, ravaged without the slightest provocation the territory of Domnall, the grandson of Ainmuireg. And from that day to this they have been trodden down by strangers—a fate which pierces the heart with sighs and grief.

CHAPTER VII.

Of the Apparition of Angels carrying to heaven the soul of the blessed Brito.

At another time while the holy man was tarrying in the Iouan island (Hy, now Iona), one of his monks called Brito, a person given to all good works, being seized with bodily illness, was reduced to the last extremity. When the venerable man went to visit him at the hour of his departure, he stood for a few moments at his bedside, and after giving him his blessing, retired quickly from the house, not wishing to see him die, and the very moment after the holy man left the house the monk closed this present life.

Then the eminent man walking in the little court of his monastery, with his eyes upraised to heaven, was for a long time lost in wonder and admiration. But a certain brother named Aidan, the son of Libir, a truly virtuous and religious man, who was the only one of the brethren present at the time, fell upon his knees and asked the saint to tell him the reason of so great astonishment. The saint said to him in reply : " I have this moment seen the holy angels contending in the air against the hostile powers ; and I return thanks to Christ, the Judge, because the victorious angels have carried off to the joys of our heavenly country the soul of this stranger, who is the first person that hath died among us in this island. But I beseech thee not to reveal this secret to any one during my life."

CHAPTER VIII.

Concerning the Vision of Angels vouchsafed the same holy man when they were bearing to heaven the soul of one named Diormit.

AT another time a stranger from Hibernia came to the saint and remained with him for some months in the Iouan island (Hy, now Iona). The blessed man one day said to him: " One of the clerics of thy province, whose name I do not yet know, is being carried to heaven by the angels at this moment." Then the brother, upon hearing this, began to search within himself regarding the province of the Anterii (Airthir), which is called in Scotic Indairthir (East Oriel, in Ulster), and also about the name of that blessed man, and in due course thus expressed himself, saying: " I know a soldier of Jesus Christ, named Diormit, who built a small monastery in the same district where I dwelt." The saint said to him, " He of whom thou speakest is the very person who hath been carried into Paradise by the angels of God."

But this fact must be very carefully noted, that our venerable man was most careful to conceal from the knowledge of men many mysterious secrets which were concealed from others, but revealed to him by God, and this he did for two reasons, as he one day hinted to a few of the brethren; first, that he might avoid vain-glory, and secondly that he might not, by the fame of his revelations being spread abroad, attract, to make inquiries at him, innumerable crowds who were anxious to ask some questions regarding themselves.

CHAPTER IX.

Of the brave fight of the Angels against the Demons, and how they opportunely assisted the Saint in the same conflict.

ON another day while the holy man was living in the Iouan island (Hy, now Iona), he went to seek in the woods for a place more remote from men and fitting for prayer. And there when he began to pray, he suddenly beheld, as he afterwards told a few of the brethren, a very black host of demons fighting against him with iron darts. These wicked demons wished, as the Holy Spirit revealed to the saint, to attack his monastery and kill with the same spears many of the brethren. But he, single-handed, against innumerable foes of such a nature, fought with the utmost bravery, having received the armour of the apostle Paul. And thus the contest was maintained on both sides during the greater part of the day, nor could the demons, countless though they were, vanquish him, nor was he able, by himself, to drive them from his island, until the angels of God, as the saint afterwards told certain persons, and they few in number, came to his aid, when the demons in terror gave way. On the same day, when the saint was returning to his monastery, after he had driven the devils from his island, he spoke these words concerning the same hostile legions, saying, "Those deadly foes, who this day, through the mercy of God and the assistance of his angels, have been put to flight from this small track of land, have fled to the Ethican land (Tiree), and there as savage invaders they will attack the monasteries of the brethren, and cause pestilential diseases, of which many will be grievously ill and die." All this came to pass in those days, as the blessed man had foreseen. And two days after he thus spake from the revelation of the Holy Ghost, "Baithen hath managed wisely, with God's help, that the congregation of the church over which he hath been appointed by God to preside, in the plain of Lunge (Magh Lunge, in Tiree), should be defended by fasts and prayers against the attacks of the demons, and but one person shall die on this occasion." The whole took place as was foretold; for whilst many in the other monasteries of the same island fell victims to that disease, none except the one of whom the saint spoke died in the congregation which was under the charge of Baithen.

CHAPTER X.

Of the Apparition of Angels whom the man of God saw carrying to heaven the soul of a blacksmith, named Columb, and surnamed Coilrigin.

A CERTAIN blacksmith, greatly devoted to works of charity, and full of other good works, dwelt in the midland districts of Scotia (Ireland). When the forementioned Columb, surnamed Coilrigin, was dying in a good old age, even at that very moment when he departed from the body, St. Columba, who was then in the Iouan island (Hy, now Iona), thus addressed a few of the senior brethren who were standing around him, "Columb Coilrigin, the blacksmith, hath not laboured in vain, seeing that he hath had the happiness, as he desired, to purchase the eternal rewards by the labour of his hands. For, behold, at this moment, his soul is carried by the holy angels to the joys of the heavenly country, because he laid out all that he could earn by his trade in alms to the poor."

CHAPTER XI.

Of a similar Vision of Angels whom the blessed man beheld carry-
ing to heaven the soul of a certain virtuous woman.

IN like manner, on another occasion, whilst the holy man was living in the Iouan island (Hy, now Iona),· he one day suddenly raised his eyes to heaven and uttered the words, " O happy woman—happy because of thy virtues ; the angels of God are now carrying thy soul to paradise." Now these words from the mouth of the saint were heard by a certain religious brother, a Saxon, by name Genere, who was at the moment working at his trade, which was that of a baker. And on the same day of the month, at the end of the same year, the saint addressed the same Genere the Saxon, and said, " I see a won-derful thing ; behold, the woman of whom I spake in thy pre-sence last year, now meeteth in the air the soul of her husband, a poor and holy man, and together with the holy angels en-gageth in a contest for it against the adverse powers; by their united assistance, and by the aid of the virtuous character of the man himself, his soul is rescued from the assaults of the demons, and brought to the place of eternal refreshment.

CHAPTER XII.

Of the Apparition of Holy Angels whom St. Columba beheld
meeting in its passage the soul of St. Brenden, the founder
of the monastery which in Scotic is called Birra (Birr, in
King's County).

ON another day also, while the venerable man was residing in the Iouan island (Hy, now Iona), he called very early in the morning for his attendant, Diormit, so frequently mentioned before, and commanded him, saying, " Make ready in haste for the celebration of the Holy Eucharist, for to-day is the birthday of blessed Brenden." " Wherefore," said his attendant, " dost thou order such solemnities of the Mass to be prepared to-day ? For no messenger hath come to us from Scotia (Ireland) to tell us of the death of that holy man." "Go," said the saint, "it is thy duty to obey my commands. For this last night I saw the heavens suddenly open, and choirs of angels descend to meet the soul of the holy Brenden; and so great and incomparable was the brightness, that in that same hour it illuminated the whole world."

CHAPTER XIII.

Of the Vision of Holy Angels who carried off to heaven the soul of the Bishop, St. Columban Mocu Loigse.

ON another day also, while the brethren were putting on their sandals in the morning, and were making ready to go to their different duties in the monastery, the saint, on the contrary, bade them rest that day and prepare for the holy sacrifice, ordering also some addition to be made to their dinner, as on the Lord's day. "I must," said he, "though unworthy, celebrate to-day the holy mysteries of the Eucharist, out of veneration to that soul which this last night went up to paradise, beyond the region of the stars in the heavens, borne thither amid the holy choirs of the angels."

At these words the brethren obeyed, and, according to his directions, rested that day; then, after preparing for the due celebration of the sacred rite, they accompanied the saint to the church in their white robes as on a festival. But it came to pass that when in the course of chanting the offices, the prayer was being sung as usual in which St. Martin's name is commemorated, the saint, suddenly turning to the chanters, when they had come to make mention of that name, said, "You must pray to-day for St. Columban, bishop." Then all the brethren present understood that Columban, a bishop in Leinster, the dear friend of Columba, had passed to the Lord. A short time after, some persons, who came from the province of Leinster, told how the bishop died in the very night in which it was thus made known to the saint.

CHAPTER XIV.

Of the Apparition of Angels who had come down to meet the souls of the monks of St. Comgell.

AT another time, when the venerable man was living in the Iouan island (Hy, now Iona), he became suddenly excited, and

summoned the brethren together by the sound of the bell.
" Now," said he, " let us help by our prayers the monks of the
Abbot Comgell, who are just now in danger of being drowned
in the Lake of the Calf (Loch Laodh, now Belfast Lough); for,
lo ! at this moment they are fighting against the hostile powers
in the air, and are striving to rescue the soul of some stranger
who is also drowning along with them."   Then after having
wept and prayed fervently, he hastily stood erect before the
altar with a joyful countenance, whilst the brethren continued
to lie prostrate in prayer.   " Give thanks," he said, "to Christ,
for now the holy angels, coming to the aid of holy souls, have
rescued this stranger from the attacks of the demons, and borne
him off in triumph like victorious warriors."

CHAPTER XV.

*Of the Manifestation of the Angels who came to meet the soul
of one Emchath.*

AT another time, when the saint was travelling beyond the
Dorsal Ridge of Britain (Drumalban), near the lake of the
river Nesa (Loch Ness), he was suddenly inspired by the Holy
Ghost, and said to the brethren that accompanied him, " Let us
go quickly to meet the holy angels, who have been sent from
the realms of the highest heaven to carry away with them the
soul of a heathen, and now wait our arrival there, that we
may baptize in due time before his death this man, who hath
preserved his natural goodness through all his life, even to
extreme old age."   And having said this much, the holy old
man hurried his companions as much as he could, and walked
before them until he came to a district called Airchart-dan
(Arochdan, now Glen Urquhart); and there he found an aged
man whose name was Emchat, who, on hearing the word of God
preached by the saint, believed and was baptized, and immediately after, full of joy, and safe from evil, and accompanied
by the angels, who came to meet him, passed to the Lord.
His son Virolec also believed, and was baptized with all
his house.

CHAPTER XVI.

Of the Angel of the Lord that came so quickly and opportunely to the relief of the brother who fell from the top of the round monastery in the Oakwood Plain (Derry).

AT another time, while the holy man sat in his little cell engaged in writing, on a sudden his countenance changed, and he poured forth this cry from his pure breast, saying, " Help! help!" Two of the brothers who stood at the door, namely, Colga, son of Cellach, and Lugne Mocublai, asked the cause of such a sudden cry. The venerable man answered, saying, " I ordered the angel of the Lord who was just now standing among you to go quickly to the relief of one of the brothers who is falling from the highest point of a large house which is now being built in the Oakwood Plain (Derry)." And the saint added afterwards these words, saying, " How wonderful and almost unspeakable is the swiftness of angelic motion, like, as I imagine, to the rapidity of lightning. For the heavenly spirit who just now flew away from us when that man began to fall, arrived there to support him, as it were, in the twinkling of an eye, before his body reached the ground ; nor was the man who fell able to feel any fracture or bruise. How wonderful, I say, is that most swift and timely help which could be given so very quickly, even though such an extent of land and sea lay between !"

CHAPTER XVII.

Of the multitude of Holy Angels that were seen to come down from heaven at the bidding of the blessed man.

ANOTHER time also, while the blessed man was living in the Iouan island (Hy, now Iona), he made this known to the assembled brethren with very great earnestness, saying, " To-day I wish to go alone to the western plain of this island ; let none of you therefore follow me." They obeyed, and he went alone, as he desired. But a brother, who was cunning, and of a prying disposition, proceeded by another road, and secretly placed himself on the summit of a certain little hill which overlooked the plain, because he was very anxious to learn the blessed man's motive for going out alone. While the spy on the top of the hill was looking upon him as he stood on a mound in the plain, with arms extended upwards, and eyes raised to heaven in prayer, then, strange to tell, behold a wonderful scene presented itself, which that brother, as I think not without the leave of God, witnessed with his own eyes from his place on the neighbouring hill, that the saint's name and the reverence due to him might afterwards, even against his wishes, be more widely diffused among the people, through the vision thus vouchsafed. For holy angels, the citizens of the heavenly country, clad in white robes and flying with wonderful speed, began to stand around the saint whilst he prayed ; and after a short converse with the blessed man, that heavenly host, as if feeling itself detected, flew speedily back again to the highest heavens.   The blessed man himself also, after his meeting with the angels, returned to the monastery, and calling the brethren together a second time, asked, with no little chiding and reproof, which of them was guilty of violating his command.   When all were declaring they did not know at all of the matter, the brother, conscious of his inexcusable transgression, and no longer able to conceal his guilt, fell on his knees before the saint in the midst of the assembled brethren, and humbly craved forgiveness. The saint, taking him aside, commanded him under heavy threats, as he knelt, never, during the life of the blessed man, to disclose to any person even the least part of the secret regarding the angels' visit. It was, therefore, after the saint's departure from the body that the brother related that manifestation of the heavenly host, and solemnly attested its truth.   Whence, even to this day, the place where the angels assembled is called by a name that beareth witness to the event that took place in it ; this may be said to be in Latin " Colliculus Angelorum " and is in Scotic Cnoc Angel (now called Sithean Mor). Hence, therefore, we must notice, and even carefully inquire, into the fact how great and of what kind these sweet visits of angels to this blessed man were, which took place mostly during the winter nights, when he was in watching and prayer in lonely places while others slept.   These were no doubt very numerous, and could in no way come to the knowledge of other men. Though some of these which happened by night or by day might perhaps be discovered by one means or another, these must have been very few compared with the angelic visions, which, of course, could be known by nobody.   The same observation applies in the same way to other bright apparitions hitherto investigated by few, which shall be afterwards described.

CHAPTER XVIII.

Of the bright Pillar seen to glow upon the Saint's head.

ANOTHER time four holy founders of monasteries came from
Scotia (Ireland), to visit St. Columba, and found him in the
Hinba island (Eilean-na-Naoimh).   The names of these distinguished men were Comgell Mocu Aridi, Cainnech Mocu
Dalon, Brenden Mocu Alti, and Cormac, grandson of Leathain.
They all with one consent agreed that St. Columba should
consecrate, in their presence in the church, the holy mysteries
of the Eucharist.   The saint complied with their express
desire, and entered the church with them on Sunday as usual,
after the reading of the Gospel; and there, during the celebration of the solemn offices of the Mass, St. Brenden Mocu
Alti saw, as he told Comgell and Cainnech afterwards, a ball of
fire like a comet burning very brightly on the head of Columba,
while he was standing before the altar, and consecrating the
holy oblation, and thus it continued burning and rising upwards
like a column, so long as he continued to be engaged in the
same most sacred mysteries.

CHAPTER XIX.

*Of the Descent or Visit of the Holy Ghost, which in the same island
continued for three whole days and nights with the venerable
man.*

AT another time, when the saint was living in the Hinba
island (Eilean-na-Naoimh), the grace of the Holy Ghost was
communicated to him abundantly and unspeakably, and dwelt
with him in a wonderful manner, so that for three whole days,
and as many nights, without either eating or drinking, he
allowed no one to approach him, and remained confined in a
house which was filled with heavenly brightness.   Yet out of
that house, through the chinks of the doors and keyholes, rays
of surpassing brilliancy were seen to issue during the night.
Certain spiritual songs also, which had never been heard before,
he was heard to sing.   He came to see, as he allowed in the
presence of a very few afterwards, many secrets hidden from
men since the beginning of the world fully revealed; certain
very obscure and difficult parts of sacred Scripture also were
made quite plain, and clearer than the light to the eye of his

pure heart. He grieved that his beloved disciple, Baithen, was not with him, because if he had chanced to be beside him during those three days, he would have been able to explain from the lips of the blessed man mysteries regarding past or future ages, unknown to the rest of mankind, and to interpret also some passages of the Sacred Volumes. However, Baithen was then detained by contrary winds in the Egean island (Egg), and he was not, therefore, able to be present until those three days and as many nights of that glorious and unspeakable visitation came to a close.

CHAPTER XX.

Of the angelic splendour of the light which Virgnous—a youth of good disposition, and afterwards made by God superior of this Church in which I, though unworthy, now serve—saw coming down upon St. Columba in the Church, on a winter's night, when the brethren were at rest in their chambers.

ONE winter's night the forementioned Virgnous, burning with the love of God, entered the church alone to pray, while the others were asleep ; and he prayed fervently in a little side-chamber attached to the walls of the oratory. After a considerable interval, as it were of an hour, the venerable Columba entered the same sacred house, and along with him, at the same time, a golden light, that came down from the highest heavens and filled that part of the church. Even the separate recess of the side-chamber, where Virgnous was striving to hide himself as much as he could, was also filled, to his great alarm, with some of the brilliance of that heavenly light which burst through the inner-door of the chamber, that was a little open. And as no one can look directly at, or gaze with steady eye on, the summer sun in his mid-day splendour, so Virgnous could not at all bear this heavenly brightness which he saw, because of the brilliant and unspeakable radiance which overpowered his sight. The brother spoken of was so much terrified by the splendour, almost as dreadful as lightning, that no strength remained in him. But, after a short prayer, St. Columba left the church. And the next day he sent for Virgnous, who was very much alarmed, and spoke to him these few consoling words : " Thou art crying to good purpose, my child, for last night thou wert very pleasing in the sight of God by keeping thine eyes fixed on the ground when thou wert overwhelmed with fear at the brightness, for hadst thou not done so, that priceless light would have blinded thine eyes. This, however, thou must carefully observe—never to disclose this great manifestation of light while I live."

This circumstance, therefore, which is so wonderful and so worthy of record, became known to many after the saint's death through this same Virgnous's relating it. Comman, sister's son to Virgnous, a respected priest, solemnly assured me, Adamnan, of the truth of the vision I have just described, and he added, moreover, that he heard the story from the lips of the abbot Virgnous, his own uncle, who, as far as he could, had seen that vision.

CHAPTER XXI.

Of another very similar Vision of great brilliancy.

ANOTHER night also, one of the brothers, whose name was Colga, the son of Aid Draigniche, of the grandsons of Fechrech mentioned in the first Book, came by chance, while the other brothers were asleep, to the gate of the church, and stood there for some time praying. Then suddenly he saw the whole church filled with a heavenly light, which more quickly than he could tell, flashed like lightning from his gaze. He did not know that St. Columba was praying at that time in the church, and after this sudden appearance of light, he returned home in great alarm. On the following day the saint called him aside and rebuked him severely, saying : "Take care of one thing, my child, that you do not attempt to spy out and pry too closely into the nature of that heavenly light which was not granted thee, but rather fled from thee, and that thou do not tell any one during my lifetime what thou hast seen."

CHAPTER XXII.

Of another like Apparition of Divine light.

AT another time also, the blessed man gave strict orders one day to Berchan, surnamed Mesloen, a pupil learning wisdom with them, saying : "Take care, my son, that thou come not near my little hut this evening, as thou art always accustomed to do." Berchan however, though hearing this, went, contrary to this command, to the blessed man's house in the dead of night while others were at rest, and cunningly put down his eyes on a line with the keyholes, in the hope that, just as the thing happened, some heavenly vision would be shown to the saint within. And at that very time the little hut was filled with a light of heavenly brightness, which the disobedient young man was not able to look upon, and therefore he fled at once from the spot. On the morrow the saint took him apart, and chiding him severely, addressed him in these words : " Last night, my son, thou hast sinned before God, and thou didst vainly imagine that the prying of thy secret inquisitiveness could be hidden or concealed from the Holy Ghost. Did I not see thee at that hour as thou didst draw near to the door of my hut, and as thou didst go away from it ? Had I not prayed for thee at that moment, thou wouldst have fallen dead there before the door, or thine eyes would have been torn out of their sockets ; but on my account, the Lord hath spared thee at this time. And be thou assured of this also, that, whilst thou art living in luxury in thine own country of Hibernia, thy face shall burn with shame all the days of thy life. Yet by my prayers, I have obtained this favour of God, that, as thou art my disciple, thou shalt do heartfelt penance before death, and thus obtain the mercy of God." All these things, according to the saying of the blessed man, occurred afterwards to him as had been foretold regarding him.

CHAPTER XXIII.

Of another Vision of Angels whom the Saint saw coming to meet his soul, as if to show that it was about to leave the body.

AT another time, while the blessed man was living in the Iouan island (Hy, now Iona), his holy countenance one day was lighted up suddenly with strange transports of joy ; and raising his eyes to heaven he was filled with delight, and rejoiced beyond measure. After an interval of a few seconds, that sweet and enchanting delight was changed into a mournful sadness.

Now, the two men, who at the same hour were standing at the door of his hut, which was built on the higher ground, and were themselves also much afflicted with him—of whom the one was Lugne Mocublai, and the other a Saxon named Pilu,—asked the cause of this sudden joy, and of the sorrow which followed. The saint said to them, " Go in peace, and do not ask me now to explain the cause of either that joy or that sadness." On hearing this they humbly asked him, kneeling before him in tears, and with faces sunk to the ground, to grant their desire of knowing something concerning that matter which at that same hour had been revealed to the saint. Seeing them so much afflicted, he said, "On account of my love to you, I do not wish you to be in sadness; but you must first promise me never to disclose to any one during my life the secret you seek to know." They made of course the promise at once according to his request, and then, when the promise was made, the venerable man spake to them thus: "On this very day, thirty years of my sojourn in Britain have been completed, and meanwhile for many days past I have been devoutly asking of my Lord to release me from my dwelling here at the end of this thirtieth year, and to call me thither to my heavenly fatherland. And this was the cause of that joy of mine, of which in sorrowful mood you ask me. For I saw the holy angels sent down from the lofty throne to meet my soul when it is taken from the flesh. But, behold now how they are stopped suddenly, and stand on a rock at the other side of the Sound of our island, evidently being anxious to come near me and deliver me from the body. But they are not allowed to come nearer, because, that thing which God granted me after praying with my whole strength—namely, that I might pass from the world to Him on this day,—He hath changed in a moment in His listening to the prayers of so many churches for me. These churches have no doubt prayed as the Lord hath granted, so that, though it is against my ardent wish, four years from this day are added for me to abide in the flesh. Such a sad delay as this was fitly the cause of the grief to-day. At the end of these four years, then, which by God's favour my life is yet to see, I shall pass away suddenly, without any previous bodily sickness, and depart with joy to the Lord, accompanied by His holy angels, who shall come to meet me at that hour."

According to these words, which the venerable man uttered, it is said, with much sorrow and grief, and even many tears, he afterwards abode in the flesh for four years.

CHAPTER XXIV.

How our Patron, St. Columba, passed to the Lord.

TOWARDS the end of the above-mentioned four years, and as a true prophet, he knew long before that his death would follow the close of that period, the old man, worn out with age, went in a cart one day in the month of May, as we mentioned in the preceding second Book, to visit some of the brethren who were at work. And having found them at work on the western side of the Iouan island (Hy, now Iona), he began to speak to them that day, saying, "During the paschal solemnities in the month of April now past, with desire have I desired to depart to Christ the Lord, as He had allowed me, if I preferred it. But lest a joyous festival should be turned for you into mourning, I thought it better to put off for a little longer the time of my departure from the world." The beloved monks all the while they were hearing this sad news were greatly afflicted, and he endeavoured as well as he could to cheer them with words of consolation. Then, having done this, he turned his face to the east, still seated as he was in his chariot, and blessed the island with its inhabitants; and from that day to the present, as we have stated in the Book above mentioned, the venomous reptiles with the three forked tongues could do no manner of harm to man or beast. After uttering these words of blessing, the saint was carried back to his monastery.

Then, again, a few days afterwards, while he was celebrating the solemn offices of the Mass as usual on the Lord's day, the face of the venerable man, as his eyes were raised to heaven, suddenly appeared as if suffused with a ruddy glow, for, as it is written, "A glad heart maketh a cheerful countenance." For at that same hour he alone saw an angel of the Lord hovering above within the walls of his oratory; and as the lovely and tranquil aspect of the holy angels infuses joy and exultation into the hearts of the elect, this was the cause of that sudden joy infused into the blessed man. When those who were present on the occasion inquired as to the cause of that joy with which he was evidently inspired, the saint looking upwards gave them this reply, "Wonderful and unspeakable is the subtility of the angelic nature! For lo, an angel of the Lord, who was sent to demand a certain deposit dear to God, hath, after looking down upon us within the church, and blessing us, returned again through the roof of the church, without leaving any trace of his passage out." Thus spoke the saint. But none of the bystanders could understand what kind of a deposit the angel was sent to demand. Our patron, however, gave the name of a holy deposit to his own soul that had been intrusted to him by God; and after an interval of six days from that time, as shall be related further on, he departed to the Lord on the night of the Lord's day. In the end, then, of this same week, that is on the day of the Sabbath, the venerable

man, and his pious attendant Diormit, went to bless the barn
which was near at hand.   When the saint had entered in and
blessed it, and two heaps of winnowed corn that were in it, he
gave expression to his thanks in these words, saying, " I heartily
congratulate my beloved monks, that this year also, if I am
obliged to depart from you, you will have a sufficient supply
for the year."   On hearing this, Diormit his attendant began
to feel sad, and said, " This year, at this time, father, thou very
often vexest us, by so frequently making mention of thy leaving
us."   But the saint replied to him, " I have a little secret
address to make to thee, and if thou wilt promise me faithfully
not to reveal it to any one before my death, I shall be able to
speak to thee with more freedom about my departure."   When
his attendant had on bended knees made the promise as the
saint desired, the venerable man thus resumed his address :
" This day in the Holy Scriptures is called the Sabbath, which
means rest.   And this day is indeed a Sabbath to me, for it is
the last day of my present laborious life, and on it I rest after
the fatigues of my labours ; and this night at midnight, which
commenceth the solemn Lord's Day, I shall, according to the
sayings of Scripture, go the way of our fathers.   For already
my Lord Jesus Christ deigneth to invite me ; and to Him, I say,
in the middle of this night shall I depart, at His invitation.   For
so it hath been revealed to me by the Lord himself."   The
attendant hearing these sad words began to weep bitterly, and
the saint endeavoured to console him as well as he could.

After this the saint left the barn, and in going back to the
monastery, rested half way at a place where a cross, which was
afterwards erected, and is standing to this day, fixed into a mill-
stone, may be observed on the roadside.   While the saint, as I
have said, bowed down with old age, sat there to rest a little,
behold, there came up to him a white pack-horse, the same that
used, as a willing servant, to carry the milk-vessels from the cow-
shed to the monastery.   It came up to the saint and, strange to
say, laid its head on his bosom—inspired, I believe, by God to
do so, as each animal is gifted with the knowledge of things
according to the will of the Creator ; and knowing that its
master was soon about to leave it, and that it would see him
no more—began to utter plaintive cries, and like a human
being, to shed copious tears on the saint's bosom, foaming and
greatly wailing.   The attendant seeing this, began to drive the
weeping mourner away, but the saint forbade him, saying :
" Let it alone, as it is so fond of me,—let it pour out its bitter
grief into my bosom.   Lo ! thou, as thou art a man, and hast a
rational soul, canst know nothing of my departure hence, ex-

cept what I myself have just told you; but to this brute beast, devoid of reason, the Creator Himself hath evidently in some way made it known that its master is going to leave it." And saying this, the saint blessed the work-horse, which turned away from him in sadness.

Then leaving this spot, he ascended the hill that overlooketh the monastery, and stood for some little time on its summit; and as he stood there with both hands uplifted, he blessed his monastery, saying:

" Small and mean though this place is, yet it shall be held in great and unusual honour, not only by Scotic kings and people, but also by the rulers of foreign and barbarous nations, and by their subjects; the saints also even of other churches shall regard it with no common reverence."

After these words he descended the hill, and having returned to the monastery sat in his hut transcribing the Psalter, and coming to that verse of the 33d Psalm (Eng. Vers. Ps. 34), where it is written, " They that seek the Lord shall want no manner of thing that is good,"—" Here," said he, " at the end of the page, I must stop; and what follows let Baithene write." The last verse he had written was very applicable to the saint, who was about to depart, and to whom eternal goods shall never be wanting; while the one that followeth is equally applicable to the father who succeeded him, the instructor of his spiritual children: " Come, ye children, and hearken unto me: I will teach you the fear of the Lord;"—and indeed he succeeded him, as recommended by him, not only in teaching, but also in writing.

Having written the aforementioned verse at the end of the page, the saint went to the church to the nocturnal vigils of the Lord's Day; and so soon as this was over, he returned to his chamber, and spent the remainder of the night on his bed, where he had a bare flag for his couch, and for his pillow a stone, which stands to this day as a kind of monument beside his grave. While then he was reclining there, he gave his last instructions to the brethren, in the hearing of his attendant alone, saying: " These, O my children, are the last words I address to you—that ye be at peace, and have unfeigned charity among yourselves; and if you thus follow the example of the holy fathers, God, the Comforter of the good, will be your Helper, and I, abiding with Him, will intercede for you; and He will not only give you sufficient to supply the wants of this present life, but will also bestow on you the good and eternal rewards which are laid up for those that keep His commandments." Thus far have the last words of our venerable patron, as he was about to leave this weary pilgrimage for his heavenly country, been preserved for recital in our brief narrative. After these words, as the happy hour of his departure gradually approached, the saint became silent. Then as soon as the bell tolled at midnight, he rose hastily, and went to the church; and running more quickly than the rest, he entered it alone, and knelt down in prayer beside the altar. At the same moment his attendant Diormit, who more slowly followed him, saw from a distance that the whole interior of the church was filled with a heavenly light in the direction of the saint. And as he drew near to the door, the same light he had seen, and which was also seen by a few more of the brethren standing at a distance, quickly disappeared. Diormit therefore entering the church, cried out in a mournful voice, "Where art thou, father?" And feeling his way in the darkness, as the brethren had not yet brought in the lights, he found the saint lying before the altar; and raising him up a little, he sat down beside him, and laid his holy head on his bosom. Meanwhile the rest of the monks ran in hastily in a body with their lights, and beholding their dying father, burst into lamentations. And the saint, as we have been told by some who were present, even before his soul departed, opened wide his eyes and looked round him from side to side, with a countenance full of wonderful joy and gladness, no doubt seeing the holy angels coming to meet him. Diormit then raised the holy right hand of the saint, that he might bless his assembled monks. And the venerable father himself moved his hand at the same time, as well as he was able—that as he could not in words, while his soul was departing, he might at least, by the motion of his hand, be seen to bless his brethren. And having given them his holy benediction in this way, he immediately breathed his last. After his soul had left the tabernacle of the body, his face still continued ruddy, and brightened in a wonderful way by his vision of the angels, and that to such a degree that he had the appearance, not so much of one dead, as of one alive and sleeping. Meanwhile the whole church resounded with loud lamentations of grief.

I must not omit to mention the revelation made to a certain saint of Ireland, at the very time the blessed soul departed. For in that monastery which in the Scotic language is called Clonifinchoil (now Rosnarea, in parish of Knockcommon, Meath), there was a holy man named Lugud, son of Tailchan, one who had grown old in the service of Christ, and was noted for his sanctity and wisdom. Now this man had a vision which at early dawn he told in great affliction to one called Fergnous, who was like himself a servant of Christ. "In the middle of this last night," said he, "Columba, the pillar of many churches, passed to the Lord; and at the moment of his blessed departure, I saw in the spirit the whole Iouan island, where I never was in the body, resplendent with the brightness of angels; and the whole heavens above it, up to the very zenith, were illumined with the brilliant light of the same heavenly messengers, who descended in countless numbers to bear away his holy soul. At the same moment, also, I heard the loud hymns and entrancingly sweet canticles of the angelic host, as his holy soul was borne aloft amidst the ascending choirs of angels." Virgnous, who about this time came over from Scotia (Ireland), and spent the rest of his life in the Hinba island (Eilean-na-Naoimh), very often related to the monks of St. Columba this vision of angels, which, as has been said, he undoubtedly heard from the lips of the old man himself, to whom it had been granted. This same Virgnous, having for many years lived without reproach in obedience amongst the brethren, led the life of an anchorite, as a victorious soldier of Christ, for twelve years more, in the hermitage of Muirbulcmar. This vision above mentioned we have not only found in writing, but have heard related with the utmost freedom by several well-informed old men to whom Virgnous himself had told it.

Another vision also given at the same hour under a different form was related to me—Adamnan—who was a young man at the time, by one of those who had seen it; and who solemnly assured me of its truth. He was a very old man, a servant of Christ, whose name may be called Ferreol, but in the Scotic tongue Ernene, of the race of Mocufirroide, who, as being himself a holy monk, is buried in the Ridge of Tomma (now Drumhome, county Donegal), amidst the remains of other monks of St. Columba, and awaits the resurrection with the saints; he said: "On that night when St. Columba, by a happy and blessed death, passed from earth to heaven, while I and others with me were engaged in fishing in the valley of the river Fend (the Finn, in Donegal)—which abounds in fish—we saw the whole vault of heaven become suddenly illuminated. Struck by the suddenness of the miracle, we raised our eyes and looked towards the east, when, lo! there appeared something like an immense pillar of fire, which seemed to us, as it ascended upwards at that midnight, to illuminate the whole earth like the summer sun at noon; and after that column penetrated the heavens darkness followed, as if the sun had just set. And not only did we, who were together in the same place, observe with intense surprise the brightness of this remarkable luminous pillar, but many other fishermen also, who were engaged in fishing here and there in different deep pools along the same river, were greatly terrified, as they afterwards related to us, by an appearance of the same kind." These three miraculous visions, then, which were seen at the very hour of our venerable patron's departure, show clearly that the Lord hath conferred on him eternal honours. But let us now return to our narrative.

After his holy soul had departed, and the matin hymns were finished, his sacred body was carried by the brethren, chanting psalms, from the church back to his chamber, from which a little before he had come alive; and his obsequies were celebrated with all due honour and reverence for three days and as many nights. And when these sweet praises of God were ended, the venerable body of our holy and blessed patron was wrapped in a clean shroud of fine linen, and, being placed in the coffin prepared for it, was buried with all due veneration, to rise again with lustrous and eternal brightness.

And now, near the close of this book, we shall relate what hath been told us by persons cognisant of the facts, regarding the above-mentioned three days during which his obsequies were celebrated in due ecclesiastical form. It happened on one occasion that a certain brother speaking with great simplicity in the presence of the holy and venerable man, said to him, "After thy death all the people of these provinces will row across to the Iouan island (Hy, now Iona), to celebrate thine obsequies, and will entirely fill it." Hearing this said the saint immediately replied : "No, my child, the event will not turn out as thou sayest; for a promiscuous throng of people shall not by any means be able to come to my obsequies : none but the monks of my monastery will perform my funeral rites, and grace the last offices bestowed upon me." And the fulfilment of this prophecy was brought about immediately after his death by God's almighty power; for there arose a storm of wind without rain, which blew so violently during those three days and nights of his obsequies, that it entirely prevented every one from crossing the Sound in his little boat. And immediately after the interment of the blessed man, the storm was quelled at once, the wind ceased, and the whole sea became calm.

Let the reader therefore think in what and how great honour our illustrious patron was held by God, seeing that, while he was yet in this mortal flesh, God was pleased at his prayer to quell the storms and to calm the seas; and again, when he found it necessary, as on the occasion just mentioned, the gales of wind arose as he wished, and the sea was lashed into fury; and this storm, as hath been said, was immediately, so soon as his funeral rites were performed, changed into a great calm. Such, then, was the end of our illustrious patron's life, and such is an earnest of all his merits.

And now, according to the sentence of the Holy Scriptures, sharing in eternal triumphs, added to the patriarchs, associated with the prophets and apostles, numbered amongst the thousands of white-robed saints, who have washed their robes in the blood of the Lamb, he followeth the Lamb whithersoever He goeth; a virgin immaculate, free from all stain, through the grace of our Lord Jesus Christ: to whom, with the Father, be honour, and power, and praise, and glory, and eternal dominion, in the unity of the Holy Ghost for ever and ever.

After reading these three books, let the diligent reader observe of what and how great merit, of what and how high honour in the sight of God our holy and venerable abbot must have been deemed worthy, how great and many were the bright visits of the angels made to him, how full of the prophetic spirit, how great his power of miracles wrought in God, how often and to what great extent, while yet he was abiding in this mortal flesh, he was surrounded by a halo of heavenly light; and how, even after the departure of his most kindly soul from the tabernacle of the body, until the present day the place where his sacred bones repose, as has been clearly shown to certain chosen persons, doth not cease to be frequently visited by the holy angels, and illumined by the same heavenly brightness. And this unusual favour hath been conferred by God on this same man of blessed memory; that though he lived in this small and remote island of the British sea, his name hath not only become illustrious throughout the whole of our own Scotia (Ireland), and Britain, the largest island of the whole world, but hath reached even unto triangular Spain, and into Gaul, and to Italy, which lieth beyond the Penine Alps; and also to the city of Rome itself, the head of all cities. This great and honourable celebrity, amongst other marks of divine favour, is known to have been conferred on this same saint by God, Who loveth those that love Him, and raiseth them to immense honour by glorifying more and more those that magnify and truly praise Him, Who is blessed for evermore. Amen.

I beseech those who wish to transcribe these books, yea, rather I adjure them by Christ, the Judge of the world, after they have diligently transcribed, carefully to compare and correct their copies with that from which they have copied them, and also to subjoin here this adjuration :—

Whoever readeth these books on the virtues of St. Columba, let him pray to the Lord for me Dorbbene, that after death I may possess eternal life.

EXPLANATION OF NAMES ON THE MAP OF IONA.

Aird,	Ard,	Height,	I., VI.
Alt a choirinn,	Alt a' chaorthainn,	Cliff [1] of the rowan,	V.
Aonaidh an taoghain,	Aonach an taghain,	Cliff of the marten,	VI.
Aonaidh mor,	An t-aonach mòr,	The great cliff,	V.
Aonaidh nan sruth,	Aonach na sruth,	Cliff of the streams,	VI.
Ard an dorain,	Aird an dobharchon,	Otter's [2] point,	IV.
Ard annraidh,	Ard annraidh,	Height of the storm,	I.
Bealach mor, an,	An bealach mor,	The great pass,	V.
Bealach nam ban,	Bealach na m-ban,	Pass of the women,	V.
Bealach nan luirgean,	Bealach na luirgen,	Pass of the legs, or shins,	V.
Beul builg,	Beul builg,	Mouth of the bag,	IV.
Beul mor,	Beul mor,	Big mouth,	VI.
Blar buidhe,	Blar buidhe,	Yellow field,	I.
Blar nam manach,	Blar na manach,	Field of the monks,	V.
Buaile nan cailleach,	Buailidh na cailleach,	Fold of the women,	V.
Caibeal Muire,	Caipeal Muire,	Mary's chapel,	I.
Cam leoib, an,	An cam leadhbh,	The crooked shed,	I.
Caolis annraidh,	Caolas annraidh,	Stormy channel,	I.
Carnan buidhe,	Carnan buidhe,	Yellow hill,	V.
Carn cul-ri Eirin, [3]	Carn cul ri Eirinn,	Carn-back-to-Ireland,	VI.
Carraig a chaolis,	Carraig an chaolais,	Rock of the channel,	VI.
Carraig mhoiltein,	Carraig a mhoiltin,	Rock of the wether,	VI.
Carraig an daimh,	Carraig an daimh,	Rock of the ox,	II.
Carraig ard annraidh,	Carraig ard annraidh,	Rock of stormy height,	I.
Carraig fada, a,	An charraig fhadha,	The long rock,	I.
Carraig na fionaig,	Carraig na fionnoige,	Rock of the scald-crow,	I.
Ceann an uird,	Ceann an uird,	Head of the mallet,	VI.
Ceann na creige,	Ceann na creige,	Head of the rock,	V.
Ceann t-sear,	Ceann t-soir,	East head,	I.
Cheapach a, [4]	An ceapach,	Plot of tillage,	III.
Chorrag, a,	An charràg,	The finger,	I.
Clacha Dubh,	Clocha dubha,	Black stones,	II.
Clachanach,	Clochanach,	Rocky ground,	I.
Clach staoin, a,	An cloch staoin,	Inclining stone,	VI.
Cladh an Diseart, [5]	Cladh an Disirt,	Cemetery of the Desert,	I.

---

[1] *Cliff.*—Alt, *ab Altitudine.*—Cormac.

[2] *Otter's.*—Dobhar-cu, 'water-hound.'

[3] *Carn-cul-ri-Eirin.*—See p. lxv, *supra.*

[4] *Cheapach.*—See Colton's Visitation

[5] *Cladh-an-Diseart.*—Cladh primarily signifies a "bank," "mound," "dike." Thus Severus's wall was called *Cladh na muice* (Irish Nennius, p. 64) ; and among the earthworks of Tara were *Nai cluid, no cluideadh gairutenn,* " Nine cluids, or rough, strong dykes" (Keneth O'Hartigan, in Petrie's Tara, p. 165). It is translated *cacumen* in the Book of Armagh ; thus where the Irish authority states, *ocus ro suidighedh Laegairi fo a sciath gaisciud fris in clod n-imechtrach n-airther descertach na rig ratha Loegairi i Temraigh,* " Laeghaire was interred with his

Cladh Chaoinich,	Cladh Chainnigh,	Cainnech's cemetery,	I.
Cladh Iain,	Cladh Iain,	Cemetery of John,	I.
Cladh nan Druineach,	Cladh na nDruidhnec,	Cemetery of the Druids,	III.
Cladh Ronain,	Cladh Ronain,	Cemetery of Ronan,	I.
Cnoc a chnu,	Cnoc a chno,	Hill of the nut,	II.
Cnocan an aiteil,	Cnoc an aiteil,	Little knoll of the prospect,	III.
Cnoc an fhiona,	Cnoc an fhiona,	Hill of the wine,	V.
Cnoc an tobair,	Cnoc an tobair,	Hill of the well,	III.
Cnoc an t-suidhe,	Cnoc an t-suidhe,	Hill of the seat,	I.
Cnoc aobhrain,[1]	Cnoc oifrinn,	Hill of the Mass,	III.
Cnoc beul moir,	Cnoc beil moir,	Hill of the big mouth,	VI.
Cnoc druidean,	Cnoc druidean,	Hill of the starlings,	V.
Cnoc fada,	Cnoc fada,	Long hill,	II.
Cnoc liathan,	Cnoc leathan,	Broad hill,	III.
Cnoc mor,[2]	Cnoc mor,	Great hill,	I.
Cnoc na carcuil,	Cnoc na carcrach,	Hill of the prison,	I.
Cnoc na cridhe,	Cnoc na cridhe or craoi,	Hill of the heart, or fold,	I.
Cnoc na faire,	Cnoc na faire,	Hill of the watching,	VI.
Cnoc na hanalach,	Cnoc na hanalach,	Hill of the panting,	IV.
Cnoc na h-uineig,	Cnoc na fuinneoige,	Hill of the window,	III.
Cnoc naingel,	Cnoc na nAingeal,	Hill of the angels,	IV.
Cnoc nan brathan,	Cnoc na m-bron,	Hill of the querns,	II.
Cnoc na meirghe,	Cnoc na meirge,	Hill of the standard,	II.
Cnoc nan carnan,	Cnoc na carnan,	Hill of the heaps,	I.
Cnoc Odhrain,	Cnoc Odhrain,	Oran's hill,	II., IV.
Cnoc urrais,	Cnoc urradhais,	Hill of surety,	II.
Corr eilean,	Corr oilean,	Heron island,	II.
Creag ghrugaig,	Creag grugach,	Frowning rock,	V.
Crois Aodhannan,	Crois Adhamnain,	Adamnan's cross,	I.
Crois Brendain,	Crois Brendain,	Brendan's cross,	I.
Crois Eoin,	Crois Eoin,	John's cross,	I.
Crois Mhairtin,	Crois Mhairtein,	Martin's cross,	I.
Crois Mic-Gilleoin,	Crois Mic-gilla-Eoin,	Maclean's cross,	I.
Crossan mor, na,	Crossana mora,	The great crosses,	I.
Cul bhuirg,	Cul bhuirg,	Back of the burgh,	II.
Currachan, an,	An currachan,	The little curach,	VI.
Dathach,[3]	Dabhach,[3]	The vat,	I.

---

shield of valour, in the external *rampart*, in the south-east of the royal rath of Laeghaire at Tara " (Petrie's Tara, p. 113); the Latin reads : "Neel pater meus non sinivit mihi credere sed ut sepelier in *cacuminibus* Temro " (fol. 10 *a b*). In another place, referring to the earthen vallum of a primitive church, it says, "Et sepelierunt eam in *cacuminibus* ecclesiæ desuper " (*ib*. fol. 14 *bb*). So "*Cacuminibus* Aisse " (*ib*. fol. 10 *aa*). In the secondary meaning of " a grave," or " burying-ground," it is very generally employed by the native Highlanders, but in this sense it is rarely used in Ireland.

[1] *Cnoc aobhrain.*—*Aiffrind* is from the Latin *offertorium*. Inchaffray, in the parish of Madderty, in Perthshire, which derives its name from this word, is latinized *Insula Missarum*. See *oifrend*, p. 305 (Orig Ed.), and *coilech n-aiffrind*, p. 239, *supra*.

[2] *Cnoc-mor.*—By a common exchange of liquids, perhaps to give more expression to the initial letter, the word *cnoc* is locally pronounced *crock*.

[3] *Dathach.*—See *dabhach*, p. cxix.

Draoinean,	Draoighnean,	Black-thorn ground,	I.
Druim an aonaidh,	Druim an aonaigh,	Ridge of the cliff,	VI.
Druim Dhugail,	Druim Dubhghaill,	Dugald's ridge,	V.
Dun Bhuirg,	Dun Bhuirgh,	Dun of the Burgh,	II.
Dun Chalbha,	Dun Chalbhaigh,	Dun of Calbha,	II.
Dun laithrichian,	Dun laithrechan,	Fort of the ruins,	VI.
Dun Mhannanain,	Dun Manannain,	Fort of Manannan,	II.
Dusgeir,	Dubh sgeir,	Black rock,	VI.
Eaglus mor,	Eclais mor,	Great church,	I.
Eala,	Ealatrom,	Bier,	III.
Eilean a' chlarsair,[1]	Oilean a chlársair,	Harper's island,	II.
Eilean annraidh,	Oileann annraidh,	Island of storm,	I.
Eilean breac,	Oilean breac,	Speckled island,	V.
Eilean carrach,	Oilean carrach,	Rough-faced island,	V.
Eilean chairbid,	Oilean charbhaid,	Chariot island,	I.
Eilean chalbha,	Oilean Chhalbaigh,	Calbha's island,	II.
Eilean didil,	Oilean didil,	Island of affection,	II.
Eilean dubh,	Oilean dubh,	Black island,	VI.
Eilean dunagan,	Oilean dunagan,	Island of knolls,	III.
Eilean Lucais,	Oilean Lucais,	Luke's island,	VI.
Eilean mhic an Ebb,[2]	Oilean mic an aba,	Island of the Abbot's son,	II.
Eilean mor,[3]	Oilean mor,	Great island,	III.
Eilean nan con,	Oilean na conn,	Island of the hounds,	II.
Eilean nan slat,	Oilean nan slat,	Island of the rods,	IV.
Eilean phort a churraich,	Oilean puirt a' curraigh,	Island of Port-a-Curach,	VI.
Fang Mhaolain,	Fang Mhaolain,	Moylan's enclosure,	V.
Farr bheann,	Far bheann,	Front peak,	V.
Garadh Eachainn,	Garadh Eachain,	Hector's garden,	VI.
Gara geal,	Garda geal,	White garden,	III.
Gart na liana,	Gort na leana,	Meadow field,	III.
Glac a phubuil,	Glac an phobail,	Dell of the people, or tent,	I.
Glas eilean,	Glas oilean,	Green island,	III.
Gleann an Teampull,	Gleann an teampull,	Glen of the church,	II.
Goirtean dubh, an,	An goirtean dubh,	The black little field,	VI.
Goirtean Iomhair,	Goirtean Iomhair,	Ivar's little field,	VI.
Iomaire an achd,	Iomaire an acta,	Ridge of the act,	I.
Iomaire nan righ,[4]	Iomaire na righ,	Ridge of the kings,	I.
Iomaire tachair,	Iomaire tachair,	Ridge of the causeway,	I.
Lag an dorain,	Lag an dobharchon,	Otter's hollow,	l.
Lag odhar,	Lag odhar,	Pale hollow,	VI.
Laithrichean,	Laithreachan,	Ruins, Sites,	VI.
Lamh odhar,	Lamh odhar,	Pale hand,	I.
Liana mhor,	Leana mhor,	Great meadow,	I.

---

[1] *Chlarsair.*—A round knoll in Culbhuirg.

[2] *Ebb.*—A round hillock in Culbhuirg.

[3] *Eilean mor.*—In Ireland there are some old compounds of *oilean*, as Ard-oilenn, but it is of rare use when compared with *Inis*. The reverse is the case in Scotland, where there is a tendency to turn *Eilean* into *Elach*, as *Elach-nave*. *Inis* seems more akin to *insula*, and *oileann* to *island*.

[4] *Iomaire nan righ.*—This name is now an *alias* for *Iomaire an tochair*, the causeway across the Lochan, but Graham applies it to the supposed ridge of royal graves in the Reilig Orain.

Liochd laithrichean, .	*Leacht laithreachan, .*	. Flag of the ruins, .	VI.
Lochan a mhanaich, .	*Lochan a mhanaigh,*	. Monks lakelet, .	III.
Lochan mor, .	*Lochan mor, .*	. Great lakelet, .	I.
Loch Staonaig,	*Loch staonaig, .*	. Lake of Staonag, .	VI.
Machar, .	*Machaire,*	. Plain, .	IV.
Maol, .	*Maol, .*	. Brow of hill, .	IV.
Maol an aonaidh,	*Maol an aonaigh,*	. Brow of the cliff, .	VI.
Maol buidhe, a,	*An mhaol buidhe,*	. The yellow hill-brow,	V.
Maol na ciche,	*Maol na ciche,*	. Brow of the pass, .	VI.
Maol nam manach, .	*Maol na manach,*	. Brow of the monks,	V.
Maol nan uain,	*Maol na n-uan,*	. Brow of the lambs,	VI.
Murlugh, .	*Murbolc,*	. Inlet of the sea,	V.
Poll dunain, .	*Poll dunain, .*	. Pool of the knoll, .	I.
Polleirinn,	*Poll Eireann, .*	. Pool of Ere, .	II.
Port a chrossain,	*Port an chrosain,*	. Port of the little cross,	I.
Port a churraich,	*Port an churraigh,*	. Port of the curach,	VI.
Port a mhuilinn,	*Port a mhuilinn,*	. Port of the mill,	I.
Port an aonaidh,	*Port an aonaigh,*	. Port of the cliff, .	VI.
Port an Diseart,	*Port an disirt,*	. Port of the Desert,	I.
Port an duine marbh,	*Port an duine mharbh,*	. Port of the dead man,	II.
Port an fhir bhreig, .	*Port an fir bhreige,*	. Port of the false man,[1]	VI.
Port ban, .	*Port ban, .*	. White port, .	II.
Port beag na Sliginnech,	*Port beag na Sligineach,*	. Little port of Sligineach,	III.
Port beul mor, .	*Port beil moir, .*	. Port of little mouth,	VI.
Port charraig an daimh,	*Port charraig an daimh,*	. Port of the ox's rock,	II.
Port cheann Aindrea,	*Port chinn Andriu, .*	. Port of Andrew's head,	IV.
Port chinn an uird, .	*Port chinn an uird, .*	. Port of the mallet head,	VI.
Port chlacha geal, .	*Port na cloch geal, .*	. Port of the white stones,	IV.
Port dunagan, .	*Port dunagain,*	. Rocky port, .	III.
Port geiltein, .	*Port gheilteain,*	. Coward's port,	IV.
Port goirtein Iomhair,	*Port ghoirteain lomhair, .*	. Port of Ivor's gort,	VI.
Port Laithrichean,	*Port Laithreachain, .*	. Port of the ruins, .	VI.
Port Loth, .	*Port Lobhtha,*	. Rotten port, .	III.
Port na cloiche,	*Port na cloich,*	. Port of the stones,	IV.
Port na Frang,	*Port na bh-Francach,*	. Port of the French,	I.
Port na marbh,	*Port na marbh,*	. Port of the dead,	II.
Port nam Mairtear,	*Port na mairtir,*	. Martyr's port,	III.
Port na muintir,	*Port na muinnter, .*	. Port of the people,	I.
Port Ronain, .	*Port Ronain, .*	. Ronan's port,	I.
Reilig Odhrain,	*Reilig Odhrain,*	. Oran's burial-ground,	I.
Ru a bheoil mhoir,	*Rubha an bheil moir,*	. Point of the big-mouth,	I.
Ru an eisg mhoir, .	*Rubha an eisc moir, .*	. Point of the big fish,	VI.
Ru na clachanach, .	*Rubha na clachanaighe,*	. Point of the stony ground,	IV.
Ru na h-aird,[2]	*Rubha an aird,*	. Point of the height,	I.
Ru na sliginnich,	*Rubha na sligineach,*	. Point of Sligineach,	III.
Ru phort na Frang, .	*Rubha poirt na bh-Francach,*	Point of Frenchmen's port,	I.

---

[1] *False man.*—So called from a tall rock supposed to resemble a man's figure.

[2] *Ru na h-aird.*—The word *rubha*, signifying "a point of land," is much more frequent in Scottish than Irish topography. *Rubha mena* was the ancient name of a point on Loch Neagh, in the county of Antrim, where the Main Water flows into that lake, now included in Shane's Castle park. There was also a *Rubha* in the Ards of the county of Down. See Reeves's Eccl. Ant. pp. 21, 379.

Ru phort nam Mairtear,	*Rubha poirt na mairtir,*	.	Point of Martyr's port, . III.
Sgeir bheag, . .	*Sgeir beag,* . . .	.	Little rock, . . . V.
Sgeir bhun an uisg, .	*Sgeir bona an uisge,*	.	Rock of water-foot, . IV.
Sgeir fir Thireidh, .	*Sgeir fir Tire-etha,* .	.	Rock of Tiree-man, . IV.
Sgeir mhor, . .	*Sgeir mor,* . .	.	Great rock, . . . V.
Sgeir nam mairt, .	*Sgeir na mairt,* .	.	Rock of the cows, . I.
Sgeir ruadh, . .	*Sgeir ruadh,* . .	.	Red rock, . . . V.
Sithean beag, . .	*Sithean beag,* . .	.	Little fairy-mound, . IV.
Sithean mor, .	*Sithean mor,* . .	.	Great fairy-mound, . IV.
Sithean mor na h Aird,	*Sithean mor na haird,*	.	Great fairy-m. of the height, VI.
Sliabh meanach, .	*Sliabh meadhonach,* .	.	Middle mountain, . II.
Sliabh siar, .	*Sliabh siar,* . .	.	The west mountain, . II.
Sliginach, . .	*Sligineach,* . .	.	Shelly ground, . . III.
Sloc dubh, . .	*Sloc dubh,* . .	.	Black gully, . . . V.
Sloc na bo duibh, .	*Sloc bo duibhe,* .	.	Gully of the black cow, . II.
Sron iolaire, .	*Sron iolair,* . .	.	Eagle's nose, . . . V.
Sruth a mhuilinn, .	*Sruth a mhuilinn,* .	.	Stream of the mill, . I.
Stac a chorr, .	*Stac a chorr,* . .	.	Stack of the raven, . II.
Stac an aonaidh, .	*Stac an aonaigh,* .	.	Stack of the cliff, . VI.
Stac liadh, .	*Stac liath,* . .	.	Gray stack, . . IV.
Stac mhic Laomain, .	*Stac mic laomain,* .	.	Mac Laomon's stack, . l.
Staonaig, . .	*Staonaig,* . .	.	Inclining ground, . VI.
Straid na marbh, .	*Straid na marbh,* .	.	Street of the dead, . l.
Teampull Ronaig, .	*Teampull Ronaig,* .	.	Ronan's church, . I.
Teanga mheanaich, an,	*An teanga meadhonach,*	.	The middle tongue, . V.
Tigh an Easbuig, .	*Tigh an easbuig,* .	.	Bishop's house, . I.
Tobar a cheathain, .	*Tobar a cheathain,* .	.	Well of the showers, . I.
Tobar mhagh Lunga,	*Tobar maighe lunga,*	.	Well of Moy-lunga, . I.
Tobar na h-aois, .	*Tobar na h-aoise,* .	.	Well of the age, . II.
Tobar Odhrain, .	*Tobar Odhrain,* .	.	Oran's well, . . I.
Tonn a mhanaich, .	*Tonn an manaigh,* .	.	Wave of the monk, . V.
Torr Abb, . .	*Tor aba,* . .	.	Abbot's pinnacle, . . I.
Tra ban nam manach,	*Traigh ban na manach,*	.	White strand of the monks, I.
Tra mor, . .	*Traigh mor,* . .	.	Great strand, . . III.
Tra na criche, .	*Traigh na criche,* .	.	Strand of the boundary, I.
Tra na siolaig, .	*Traigh na siolaig,* .	.	Strand of the sand-eel, . III.
Tra an t-suidhe, .	*Traigh an tsuidhe,* .	.	Shore of the seat, . . I.
Uamh a bhodaich, .	*Uamh an bhodaigh,* .	.	Oldman's, or clown's, cave, V.
Uamh an t-seididh, .	*Uamh an t-seididh,* .	.	Cave of the puffing,[1] . V.
Uamh chrossain, .	*Uamh an chrosain,* .	.	Cave of the little cross, . V.
Uamh na Caisg, .	*Uamh na Caisg,* .	.	Cave of Easter, . VI.
Uamh nan calmam, .	*Uamh na colman,* .	.	Cave of the pigeons, . V.
Uamh nan sgarbh, .	*Uamh na sgarbh,* .	.	Cave of the cormorants, V.
Uiridh riomhach, an,	*An uiridh riomhach,*	.	The fine dell, . . VI.

---

[1] *Puffing.*—See the description of the Spouting Cave in Graham's Iona, p. 26, and plate 51. Mac Swyne's Gun on the coast of Donegal presents a similar, but much more powerful, action.